MW01706610

CONCUSSION

WENDY CLAWSEY

CONCUSSION

Canadian Cataloguing in Publication Data
ISBN 978-0-9920-128-0-9

Cover Art and Marketing
hot PINK boots

Editing and Pre-Press
words ... along the path
a branch of One Thousand Trees

Printed and bound in Canada

I am incredibly grateful to my daughter Maya for igniting the flame for writing within me; a flame that cannot be extinguished.

To my dear friend Doug. Without you the fog would not have lifted and I would not be able to turn around and help others. Your kindness and generosity has provided me with a second chance for health and happiness. I will always be grateful and thankful for you in my life.

Jeff Hicks from The Record, for writing your article that inspired this book, 'Life After The Fall: A single mom rediscovers herself post-concussion'. Thank you!

Lisa Browning, thank you for believing in this project even when I was feeling doubtful. I am honoured to be one of your writers.

To find the supplements mentioned in this book, please go to www.wendyclawsey.com.

Doctors go to school to learn how to cure disease and how to make people feel more comfort once they have acquired an illness. The advice in this book is not intended to replace your medical adviser. It is recommended that you check with your medical adviser before starting any new health regimen. The recommendations in this book have been provided to help you aid your doctor by becoming the healthiest version of yourself that you can be.

CONTENTS

FOREWORD

Wendy Clawsey had it all; a great life and family accompanied by a happy-go-lucky attitude. This changed instantly while she was skiing and suffered a concussion from a fall. Being concussed, she dealt with denial, a roller coaster ride of emotions and a wide array of various symptoms. Her life was turned upside down, never knowing from one moment to the next who she would be or how she could keep her post-concussion symptoms hidden. She existed in the land of "lost and misfit toys".

Suffering from a concussion can consume your life. Acknowledgment of life limiting symptoms and acceptance of limitations can be difficult to deal with, but dealing with both is integral to full recovery. Trying to continue life as it was, prior to a concussion, can actually impede the healing process. Recovery can be a long journey that your brain and body must take together in tandem.

Concussion is an invisible injury, unlike a broken limb. Upon visual inspection from others you may appear to be completely fine. However you are broken and sadly, with concussions, you will either completely heal or you will suffer from devastating repercussions. There is no set timeline to resuming a normal life without symptoms. Despite the similarity to others who have suffered the same, the complexity of returning to a state of normalcy following concussion can differ greatly.

Wendy's book covers the canvas of concussion in great detail as she paints a portrait of her long and difficult journey as a victim of post-concussion syndrome. Hers was a bumpy road to recovery. Wendy offers many healthy alternatives to explore and shares her experiences during recovery and afterwards with PCS. She explains that a healthy mind and body won't prevent a concussion, but can help smooth the road along the way to recovery and help you return to a life that you could find acceptable.

Dave Ferguson
Talk Radio Host
Beyond the Cheers
www.beyondthecheers.com

ABOUT THE BOOK

Part One is a true story based on one woman's struggle to find her way back from a life-shattering head injury. A true riches to rags to self-enlightenment story.

Part Two deals with the issues surrounding health in the same sensible and realistic way Wendy viewed her health as she was trying to recover. It is not intended to replace your medical adviser. It is intended for those who are looking for good health by using the laws of Nature, rather than the newest fads, who wish to get healthy for the sake of themselves and their loved ones. It is for those who have neither the time nor the desire to delve deeply into the study of health for themselves, and wish to follow the lead of someone who has traveled the path of learning and has created a plain and simple course of action. Keeping the information basic, without any excess, so that all can understand the simplicity that the body truly represents.

The reader is asked to set aside all pre-conceived notions of how to obtain health and to take the guidance shared here on faith. Those who take action, and follow the advice to the letter, will find themselves healthier and happier for it. The body is incredibly intelligent and will indeed perform at its highest level when it is given the proper tools -- just as a mechanic, a doctor, or a surgeon can perform at their best only when they are provided with the tools of their trade.

Part Three contains a health questionnaire, a journal in which to keep track of your daily activities and goals, and some healthy recipes to get you started!

Part One

Nothing Left to Lose

CHAPTER ONE

Nothing can put life more into perspective than losing everything!

Everything I thought I knew, everything I had and expected out of life, smashed and crumpled around me. My friends, my family, and my career gone in the time it would take a butterfly to flutter its wings, a bee to draw nectar, and a shooting star to disappear into the night sky.

After the darkness filled my head and I awoke, my thoughts were not about my family, as I always took great care in that department.

My first thought was, "What am I doing with my life?"

Little did I know at the time, I was destined to lose everything.

Lifting my face out of the snow, I struggled to come back from the in-between world I had just been in. Sometimes I wonder if, had I not opened my eyes, that would have been it. The end of my life. Was I granted more time on this Earth for a reason? Am I to learn something? Give something? Or receive something? If struggles are a teaching instrument for us to learn, then I was about to learn the lesson of a lifetime.

As I spun back into reality, the confusion that surrounded me attacked like an unannounced enemy. My head felt like it was being squeezed in a tight grip. People glided up to me, talking and asking questions. But I couldn't hear the words or understand why I was there. As I struggled to make sense of the chaos, I looked up the snow covered hill. About twenty feet away, someone was picking up a ski that was familiar to me. Yes! That's it, I had been skiing.

***

The morning had begun like any other. My eyes fluttered open minutes before my alarm, set to go off at 6:00 am. Looking out the window, I saw the mud-filled streets. The mild winter had left everything wet and damp. Pulling on my running gear, my chocolate lab thumped his tail on my bedroom floor with anticipation of our daily run.

Feeling the pavement under my feet, I inhaled deeply, taking in the morning aroma.

The calm, quiet mornings were a treasured treat for me. Feeling my blood pump and watching the sun rise as I made my way through our neighbouring streets, I felt proud knowing that I was ready for my first marathon in the fast-approaching summer of 2009. My chocolate lab, Bailey, happily kept pace beside me, and our black and white cat, Sylvester, followed us from a distance.

Glancing up just in time to witness the fleeting gold-rimmed clouds, I smiled softly to myself. This was the first day I had off in some time. Although the recession had hit and my company's competitors were not selling homes in the surrounding sites, my partner and I were selling out. Close to ten homes a month. In order to keep up with demands, the builder had to hire a second site supervisor. Things were good. No, great. My twelve year old daughter and I were about to take a day trip to Blue Mountain, a two-hour drive away, to spend the day skiing. She wanted to get one more day in on her new skis that season, and I was more than happy to oblige.

After finishing my run, I poured myself a large glass of cold water. I felt the coolness glide down my throat as I entered my daughter's bedroom. We had just redone her room in a soft blueberry-coloured paint, new solid wood white dressers from the local Mennonite store, new drapes, and bed cover, accented with matching pillows. She looked so peaceful, her blonde hair falling softly beside her angelic face. There is nothing quite like the serenity of a child tucked safely under their covers, silently sleeping.

Sitting down on the edge of the bed, I didn't want to disturb her. I could have spent the day watching her slumbering. When she was an infant, I would take advantage of those still moments to make a pencil sketch of her, always telling myself that, when I found the time, I would convert the image into a painting. Yet the time kept passing, and she kept growing, and nothing ever stopped long enough for my creations to take shape.

I softly nudged her and whispered her name, "Maya, it's time to wake up. We have a big day ahead of us."

Her sleepy eyes parted slightly as her arms reached out and around my waist. She lifted her head and snuggled it onto my lap.

"Five more minutes, please Mom."

I cupped my hand on her soft cheek and smiled down at her. I couldn't help but reflect on how lucky I was to have such an incredible child. Snuggling down beside her, I too feel asleep. Waking late, we quickly got up and ready. We stopped on the way to the ski hill for coffee and breakfast to eat on the road.

Maya inherited my silly gene and we often had moments of light-hearted fun that really made no sense to others; however, they sent us flying into fits of blissful laughter. With the anticipation of the fun-filled day on the hills, that morning was particularly silly. Maya, standing beside the car as I pulled out our skis, felt an urge of gayness and decided to express it by making funny faces at herself in the side mirror of the car. At that precise moment, someone drove past and caught her in her moment of bizarreness. As he pinched his brows and glanced at her as if she was insane, we both fell into a fit of laughter.

With our stomachs in stitches and our faces hurting from laughing, we headed for the hills. Run after run, we zipped down the ski hill with the wind nipping at our noses. I was laughing at Maya as the sun glistened in the snow and she sped past, pointing and laughing at me.

I bent my knees, lifted my poles and leaned forward. As I started to gain speed, the biting air was brisk on my face. I would soon catch up to her. She smiled at me as she looked back and then started to go even faster. Leaning in, I tried to gain more speed. Then it happened. My left ski scraped and snagged on a rough patch of unplowed ice. I looked down.

Shit! was all I had time to think.

The movies have it right; everything does seem to slow down at moments of danger as your faculties become fully focused on the impending doom. I witnessed my ski pop off as it stayed behind on the ice and my body continued to move. Then there was a fierce smash to the back of my skull, like a sledgehammer being swung with debilitating force. Everything went black.

***

What am I doing with my life? was my first and only thought before the blackness faded completely away.

I often wonder if this thought was a gift planted in my head to wake me up and remind me to live my life with purpose.

My focus drifted in and out, like the lens of a camera. Spots of light started to shine brightly against the darkening sky. Things and people were moving, talking, but I couldn't make sense of what it all was or what was being said.

Slowly the images and the sounds started to merge into one coherent scene. Life itself seemed to be playing out from some big movie projector, and I was the sole audience. Half living in the world, and half living out of it.

As I became aware of my surroundings, I noticed the people gathered around. I couldn't understand why they were all there, just watching and looking down at me.

"Are you okay?" A stranger asked.

Glancing up at him, I tried to make sense of what he just said. It seemed strange that he was talking to me. Looking high in the sky, I watched as the chair-lift kept moving upward. *I think I was on that,* I thought to myself.

"Are you okay?" the stranger asked again.

Turning back to him, I finally managed to mumble, "Yes." Not because I was; I wasn't sure what I was, or what had happened. It's just what we are programmed to say when someone asks how we are. No one really wants, or expects, to hear the truth. If you dare to say you're having a bad day, they stand there wishing they never asked.

"Are you sure?"

Looking down at the white, fake snow, I picked some up and crushed it in my glove. It felt more like little shards of glass than snow, but its temperature was still the same. The coldness slowly crept over my body, but I couldn't seem to move to get out of it.

Glancing around again, I noticed the people standing there, more of them looking at me. Like an exhibit on display. Not saying anything, only staring in wonder. Past them and up the hill, someone was picking up my ski. Others, in opposite directions, were picking up my poles.

All the while, my head was feeling as if it was being crushed in a vice grip. I removed my hat and goggles and tied them around my wrist, but it did nothing to ease the pain.

"Are you here with someone?" a lady with a soft voice asked.

Maya! Tears started to build in my eyes. *Where is she? She must be so scared!*

"My daughter."

"It's okay, I'll go get her. Do you know where she is?" the lady's kind eyes were reassuring.

"Probably waiting for me at the bottom."

"Will she come with me?"

What was that word? Our safe word for when we were separated. What was it; why didn't we go over the safe word again since she was a young child?

After telling her Maya's name, I watched as she skied away. I felt helpless not being able to get to my daughter and tell her I was alright. She must be so scared. I wanted to move, but my head was hurting far too much.

My hat, it's too tight. I tried desperately to get my hat off. *Why won't it come off?*

The man started to stare at me strangely as my hands were on my head, attempting to remove my hat. *Why does my head hurt so much and why won't my hat come off? It's so tight!* The pain was unbearable, and it was all I could think about at that moment. Looking down at my hands, I realized that my goggles were wrapped around my wrist with my hat tucked in the band. *How did they get there?*

Snow crunched loudly as a ski patrol glided up to me with her ski gurney trailing behind.

"Are you okay?"

"Yes."

"Do you want to get in the gurney?"

Oh God no, that would be embarrassing, more people would stare. I responded with a definite "No!"

I looked around, trying to find Maya. *Where is she? Why isn't Maya here with me?* Then I remembered. *That's right, the lady, she went to get her. But what if something happened to her, I can't move, not just yet. My head hurts too much.* The pain was crippling. I lifted my hands to my head once again. *I have to get my hat off. Why is it so tight?*

"Are you sure?"

What? Who is that? Oh, the ski patrol. "Yes, I'm fine."

Then I saw Maya. Her face was white and full of worry. Her eyes had laser-beam focus as she inspected me up and down. She smiled at me, but I could tell she was holding in her tears.

"Mom?" she said with a slight quiver.

I have to play it cool; I need to show Maya that everything is okay. Seeing Maya forced me to push myself to get up. We finally managed to ski down the remainder of the hill and to the chalet to get our things to go home. But we never made it home that night. Nausea hit me hard and everything started to turn. I had no choice; as much as I wanted to shrug off the bizarre feeling I was having and protect Maya, I informed a worker at the chalet of my condition. An ambulance soon arrived. At this point, all I remember is being confused about the date and hearing Maya tell the paramedics not to listen to me, when I said I was okay.

"She'll say that, even if she's not."

***

My body temperature dropped to an unbearable low, and all the blankets in the ambulance couldn't warm me. I could feel my body shaking feverishly, as I was strapped onto the board with my neck in a brace.

"You're our thirteenth head injury today," the paramedic explained. "You're lucky; one guy's helmet cracked in half when he hit a tree, not to mention Natasha Richardson three days ago."

"Who?" I asked.

"The actress who died from hitting her head while learning to ski."

How did I not hear about that? I wondered.

"I've been skiing since I was five," I tried to explain.

"You should still wear a helmet."

With the rotating landscape came an unsettling feeling in my stomach. The remnants of my meal tried to work their way back up. All the while, the throbbing in the back of my head continued to invade.

"What year is it?" the paramedic asked.

Oh God, not again, not another question. Is it 2001? No, that's not right! But what year is it, then?

Looking up, I saw Maya's smiling face. She seemed fine. *Good, she's not worried. I have to keep it that way. Okay, what year is it? I asked myself. Think, you need to figure this out for Maya. It can't be 2001, because Maya was born in 1997 and she's twelve. That's right. So 2002, no. 2003. No. 4? No, no, no...*

The paramedic's smile vanished as she leaned forward and looked at me. That worry and concern is imprinted in my mind, as it reflected the mirror image of what I was feeling inside at that precise moment.

Shit, shit, shit! I can't let her know I don't know. Think! It's not 2007, or 8. 9? No. 10? Wait! 9, it's 2009! I think? That feels right somehow!

"2009?"

As the paramedic's concern melted away, I knew I had it right and relief flowed over me. I did it. *Maya will never know that something is just not right. She can't; it will destroy her.*

Lying on the hard surface of the paramedic's board was difficult. Having my head and body strapped down, unable to move, was frustrating. Yet, not as grueling as the savage pain on the back of my head. Curling my toes and gripping my fists, I did everything I could to hide the agony I was in from my daughter. Until I couldn't hold it in any longer, and tears slipped out the corners of my eyes.

"Mommy?"

"I'm fine, darling. My head just hurts, that's all."

"I'm going to get someone."

"No, no, I'm fine, stay with me."

Lying on the hospital bed alone and waiting for Maya to return felt far too long. Little did I know at the time, that would be the state I would be in for the next few years to follow. Sleeping twenty hours a day for over six months, unable to even walk down the hall of my home, without needing to rest. The spinning, nauseous, leaden feeling that would consume me and prevent me from living a normal life was to be my unfortunate reality for years to come.

CHAPTER TWO

The haze in my head was soft at first, like a light snow drifting through the air on a breezy winter day. My thoughts, although somewhat of a kaleidoscope of mismatched pieces, were fairly coherent the day after my accident. My feelings remained well intact and light. With a long overdue weekend off, I wanted to have some fun! After all, if we were going to be trapped in Blue Mountain for a few days, we might as well make the best of it.

"Let's go skiing!" I beamed with excitement.

"No, mom!"

"Why?"

"Because you had an accident."

"Oh, yeah. I forgot."

It's strange how life works. I would have loved to have the weekend off to spend it with Maya at a ski resort. But not like that! Not being able to do anything, restricted to our room. Restlessness and confinement started to take over. After a couple of days, I assured myself I was finally okay to drive home.

"Please sir, can I have some more?" Maya held a bowl up to me, pretending to be Oliver Twist. A little actress in the making.

Raising my left eyebrow, I warned jokingly, "If you don't let me get our things together..." Then changing my facial expression to an intense stare, I hunched my back and inched my way towards her. In a hackling voice, I mimicked the wicked witch from The Wizard of Oz, "I'll get you, my pretty, and your little dog, too!" My wiggling fingers announced a pending tickle attack. Maya screamed and giggled before running around the room in a fake attempt to get away. Letting me catch her, we fell onto the bed, laughing and giggling.

Moments later, my body relaxed as I slipped in behind the steering wheel, the feeling of home warming my thoughts. Looking over at Maya, we smiled softly at each other. She felt it too. There really is no place like home.

"I can't wait to get home and see Dooley and Sylvester!" Maya announced.

"Me too."

Life and its little experiences are so precious. The smallest things like the excitement when you're finally off for that anticipated vacation and the blissfulness of returning home. These are the moments that sometimes slip our attention, but those wonderful experiences should be savoured and adored. They are as much a part of life as the trip in its entirety.

Maya leaned back in the car and stretched her arms over her head. The noise her hands made as they softly rubbed against the velvet on the roof of the car screeched in my ears with an unbearable sensation. Similar to nails on a chalkboard. Only times one hundred, in irritation level.

"Don't do that!" I snapped.

"What?" Maya asked with bewilderment.

Clinching my teeth and digging my nails into the leather of the gear shift, "Your hands! Don't do that!"

"Okay," she agreed quietly.

I watched as she then leaned forward and turned on the radio. We would normally blare the music and sing at the top of our lungs on our road trips, without any care to how we looked to those on the outside of the car. In fact, it was quite amusing to watch people's faces as they watched us.

As her hand reached forward and turned the radio up, the music hammered my eardrums. My initial reaction was to cover my ears before turning the radio down.

"Don't touch it!" I snapped.

"But I can't hear."

Turning the volume down to level one, the music flowed softly and was bearable to me. Although, now I wonder how that was possible, as I can no longer hear the music at that level.

"It's loud enough!" I said.

There it was. The first time I would see that look of perplexity on someone's face and I would be left wondering why they were looking at me that way. Leaving me trying to figure out what I said or did that was so wrong.

As a new homes sales rep, I always said, "The only international language is body language." If you look at someone as if they are your next paycheque, guess what? They will feel like you're after their money. If you care about them and wonder how you could help them create their dream home, they will feel as if you care, because you intrinsically do.

It was people's body language that would speak to me in volumes, to let me know I was saying or doing something that was not quite right. I wouldn't be able to understand what I was doing wrong. Regardless, I would know my actions were questionable and it would confuse me even more.

"I'm sorry," I said sadly.

I couldn't understand what was starting to happen to me, and I wanted to cry at my beautiful little girl's reaction to my odd behaviour.

"It's okay mom, I get it!" Just like that, her soft smile melted my heart and made me feel better.

We silently made our way home.

***

The world became topsy-turvy; nothing sat straight anymore. It spun, it turned, it twisted, and I was stuck on the ride, with no way off. Noises became louder, lights shone too brightly, and everything moved far too quickly.

The birds that I once loved to hear in the morning became wretched little devils I wanted to shoot with a pellet gun. When my sister annoyed me, I wanted to rip her head off and feed it to the dog. But then there was that girl. My daughter, who sat quietly beside me as I slept, somehow made me remember who I was. I knew I loved her, but that feeling I had for her before the accident happened, the one that made my heart melt every time I saw her -- that feeling was disconnected somehow. Lost in a maze of confusion and fog.

Sitting half in the world, and half out of the world, gave me a whole new perspective. *This is what serial killers must feel like! I thought to myself, Half dead inside, not giving a shit about anyone or anything.* That numb feeling I had still gives me shivers to this day.

I remember walking with my daughter after the accident. Not far; I had just made it past the one block mark. She did something; I don't even know what. But, I must have said something mean or yelled. Because the next thing I remember, she whipped her head around. Her eyes were as wide as saucers as she stared at me, speechless, either with fear or hurt, or perhaps both. All I thought was, I don't think I talk to her this way. Yet, even with that realization, I felt nothing for her!

All the feelings I had, all the care and worry for others, vanished. It was as if the magic strings that kept others attached to my heart were cut and I was no longer an instrument to be played in the game called humanity and love.

I was cold and dead inside, and it was somewhat of a relief to me.

"I don't give a shit about anyone or give a damn what they think anymore," I remember telling someone, "and it feels great!"

The weight of the world, all that empathy I normally felt, lifted from my shoulders, and I felt free. Yet there she was, the me before the accident, watching and waiting. In moments of quiet and stillness, my old me would slip back in. *Remember,* she would whisper to me, *remember that you care, remember who you are.*

Then again, the whipping and turning of the world. Everything in my head firing at once. Having to plug my ears to watch a movie. Talking, talking, everyone talking and moving and cluttering and clanging everywhere. It was all too much!

"Are you sure the doctor said you can drive?" my dad asked.

"Yeah, why wouldn't he?"

"You came to a complete stop!"

"And?"

"You looked both ways."

"So?"

"You never come to a complete stop!"

I glared at him. *Are you trying to piss me off? Don't you know that, every time I turn my head, everything starts to spin and spin, and won't stop?* The faster I looked to the right and then to the left, the more quickly the world twirled around me. I thought he should know that I moved my head gingerly to keep the tormenting twisting of the world to a minimum.

***

As if it wasn't enough that I was living in a world that could be compared to an Alfred Hitchcock movie, with its twisted endings and gripping plots, there was no need for special effects or mood setting music. The obscure and bizarre world I seemed to be looking out at was more than enough to send tingles up anyone's spine. I couldn't even seem to pull my intelligence together enough to work the once familiar self-checkout machine at the grocery store.

All of a sudden, I was an infant, learning, testing, and trying everything for the first time. It pissed me off, and people pissed me off.

I kept pushing the buttons, but the machine kept fighting me. Asking me stupid questions in a volume that was too loud and piercing my eardrums.

"Do you have any coupons?" it asked in a musical tone.

Why won't the stupid machine just let me ring my fucking food through? The damn fucking idiot people who designed this stupid frigging thing should be shot!

As I was getting more and more flustered, the girl in charge of all the checkout machines noticed something was wrong.

Who does she think she is, looking at me as if I'm some kind of crazy person?!

She stared at me, most likely trying to figure out what was wrong with me. I could see it in her eyes -- puzzlement and wonder. I had seen it often in others since the accident. Perhaps, if blood was oozing out of my head, people would have offered assistance instead of judgment. I waited for someone to tell me that everything would be okay, and that I didn't have to struggle alone, that they understood what was going on in my head. However, my signs of injury were invisible and I couldn't communicate well enough to explain, so help was never fully offered.

"It's not working!" I stammered. It wasn't enough that my thoughts were obscured. The ones I did have, I verbalized with difficulty. Most of the time, my thoughts and words simply got trapped in my head with no hope of escape. This too pissed me off and made me irritable.

"If you just..." the checkout girl tried to say in a voice that she would use towards a child.

"No!" Slamming everything down, "Why do you have such stupid machines here anyways?!" I snapped before I stumped off, leaving my much-needed groceries behind.

Sitting in my car, I cried. I knew I shouldn't have tried to do the laundry and shopping all in one day. It was far too much! Yet so much time had gone by and I couldn't stand being helpless anymore. I was once full of life and energy; now I was nothing more than a burden to all those around me. A broken and cracked version of the person I once was.

Gripping the steering wheel in my clenched, white-knuckled fists, I stomped my feet on the car floor with frustration. I could feel my body tingling and shaking, my head whirling with confusion.

***

Moments of time seemed to slip through my reality like a magic trick at the circus. One minute, something happened, the next minute I forgot. Lost in the maze of wacky mirrors and obscured reflections, I was unable to find my way out. Then, as if a trap door swung open, I started free-falling with no end in sight.

My anger and hostility towards others kept pushing everyone away. My relationships fell to pieces. Only those who truly knew who I was stayed and suffered alongside me. I did my best to hide my new reality from others, keeping my visits short, and only when I was well-rested. I was unable to control all situations, and there were times when the cracks in my personality showed through.

"I hate you, I hate you, I hate you! You're such a stupid little brat and you only care about yourself. I can't stand you, I only tolerate you because you're my sister. But really, I fucking hate you!" I screamed at my sister with no remorse.

Sending daggers at her with my eyes, I tried to will her away. *Why won't she go the fuck away and let me sleep?!*

My youngest sister Jordan got the brunt of my brain-injured hostility. I can only imagine it's because she was around more often than others and living with me in her own part of the house. Although we got along like two peas in a pod and had a lot of fun together, she annoyed me like only younger siblings can. Amplified by feelings made stronger yet obscured by my concussion; she unfortunately got more than her fair share of my unkindness.

"Wendy, that's enough." I remember hearing my dad say.

"It's like she doesn't have an on off switch," my other younger sister Mary-Jo stated.

I can still see everyone's faces to this day, looking at me in puzzlement.

Fine, hate me! Gang up on me and hate me. See if I fucking care! I hate all of you too!!! All I could feel was anger. I was trapped in a broken mind and body, with my thoughts criss-crossing and getting jumbled up along the way, with no one who understood, and all who, I thought, condemned and hated me. Feeling as if I was constantly on the defense from hostile intruders made for a very scary and dark time.

God, please! When will I be normal again? Over and over, again and again, I asked, I begged, and I pleaded. But the answer never came. I wept and begged for an end. Maybe waking up on that hill wasn't such a precious gift after all.

CHAPTER THREE

Near the end of the fall of 2007, two and a half years before my accident, when my mind was well intact, my life and money were flowing smoothly. I had an unquenchable thirst to open Maya up to the world and everything it had to offer. From front-row seats at the Raptors, to the ballet, art galleries, the symphony and museums, I wanted her to drink from all the cups that life had to offer. The only way to find out one's passions, likes, and dislikes is through experience.

The mood hit me, and I decided to take Maya to her first Broadway show. I extended the invitation to Jordan, and we all headed arm in arm to New York City.

"What should I pack for New York?" Maya asked, excited for her first trip to the Big Apple.

"Warm clothes and comfortable shoes," I replied practically.

The smell and the smog of New York City still courses through my veins. Even though I had lived there for only four months while modeling at nineteen, I will never forget the magical summer of bright lights and champagne parties, with bottomless cups.

Maya grinned, "What are we going to wear to the show?"

I could see the familiar glitter sparkling in her eyes. That shine of excitement that comes from the anticipation of visiting a new place. Especially one that holds so much promise for a good time. I loved to see that sparkle in her eye!

I pulled out a couple of outfits, casual nice for the show, and held them up to her. Maya frowned.

Unfortunately, most people don't get dressed up for shows anymore. But Maya had something else in mind. So I did what any good mother would do. I stayed up all night and made dresses for us to wear. From pattern to dress, I did it all. It felt good to use my dressmaking skills again. Something I did not have to do in a long time, not with the money I was making selling houses. I could buy any outfit I wanted. Yet somehow it was fun making them from scratch when it was more for pleasure than necessity.

Maya's going to love this, I thought, pulling out the fabric from a pile of material I had tucked away.

Before the accident, I could stay up all night and still have energy to spare. I was always going and doing without running out of steam. In my down times, I loved to read. I would pull out my old books from university and stay up all night reading. It could be Psychology, Neurology, Criminology, it didn't matter. I just loved to learn. I would read medical journals with thirst-quenching pleasure. My new-found interest in business books also kept me busy. Reading books like *Good to Great, The Tipping Point,* and so on. For pure pleasure, it was *War and Peace* or *Anna Karenina* by Leo Tolstoy. It was difficult to find modern fiction that would please my palate after such classics.

As everyone slumbered, my machine kept up its rhythm of song, as it stitched along the delicate fabrics. I styled my black and red dress after one I saw in a fashion magazine.

Maya woke to a satin pink dress covered in sheer pink chiffon. Her dreams of hitting the Big Apple in style panned out. She squealed with delight and jumped out of bed.

"Thank you, thank you, thank you!" She hugged me tight, then rushed to try it on.

She looked like a princess as she twirled, looking at herself in the mirror with admiring eyes. I also thought of Jordan. Although I didn't have time to make three dresses, I took one of my dresses and altered it to fit her style. We would all go to the ball adorned in our new gowns.

After a short flight to New York City, our car pulled up to the Waldorf Astoria. I couldn't help but remember the run-down model apartment I lived in on the corner of 34th and Broadway. It was anything but luxurious but, at the time, it was the penthouse to me. Living with three other models, all of us young and full of big dreams. It was a magical time, one I wish that I had the maturity to fully appreciate.

However, I must admit, entering the Waldorf with its marble floors and gold-trimmed decor, I was very thankful that the times of cheap food and knock-off hand bags were over. Nothing but butter-silk leather and luxury clothing for me, with my regular manicures and facials to keep me looking fresh and impeccable.

Since my career as a New Homes Sales Rep, I became a hotel snob. I felt that the experience of the place we stayed at, as well as the food and ambience, made the trip. I decided to splurge for a three-day long weekend at the Waldorf. The luxury Waldorf Astoria met every one of our expectations. Elegant chandeliers hanging from the ceiling. Vases larger than Maya, filled with fresh-cut flowers and displayed on oversized tables. Everything seemed to shine with grandeur.

As our stilettos clicked over the sparkling marble floors, we made our way to the concierge after checking in. Three priceless tickets to a night of unquestionable bliss were waiting for us. As a young and starving model, I had walked past the signs for Phantom of The Opera all summer long and dreamed of the day I would be able to watch the show. Now, not only was I going to be able to watch it, I would be sharing it with two people I loved and adored more than life itself. I could just imagine the ear-to-ear smiles, the giddy laughter, and the eager anticipation as we waited for the curtains to rise.

Almost breathless, I walked up to the concierge with his snobbish and self-important air. My broad smile gave away my unaccustomed, eager expectations for the evening's affair.

"You have three tickets under Wendy Clawsey."

"I'm sorry to tell you, the show has been cancelled."

"Pardon?"

"The stage hands went on strike a few hours ago and the show has been cancelled."

It can't be! The whole purpose of our trip was the show. With heavy steps, we looked around for the private elevators to the upper floors; our floor's concierge showed us to our room.

"Will there be anything else?"

"No thank you."

After giving him what was most likely an insignificant tip, as we never saw him again, we were left alone to contemplate our evening. However, once stepping out of our hall and into our room, we did not dwell long. The lush draperies that hung with exact precision, the pillow-topped bed with its double sheeting, and the elegant furnishings pleased our eyes.

"Oh, wow!"

Maya squealed, jumped on the oversized bed, and started to bounce. I'll have to admit, she wasn't the only one!

As air came between our feet and the bed, our light-hearted laughter resonated through the room. Our long weekend of unplanned fun had begun. Shopping, horse-drawn buggy through Grand Central Park, and fine cuisine were all amongst our trip's activities.

We also had access to the private lounge at the Waldorf, where we were served a breakfast every morning consisting of cold cuts, fresh fruits, and pastries. Our coffee was served out of silver urns into our china cups. Throughout the day, it was a place to rest after our shopping excursions, and receive refreshments. Before dinner, hors d'oeuvres were served, and a young lady was always available at her desk to assist us with any of our New York needs.

On the day of our departure, we arrived at the airport far too late. A young man with a soft voice was more than happy to help us. He escorted us past the line at customs and helped us rush through.

"When you get through, run. Go down that hall, turn right, and follow it until you get to your terminal. Don't stop running or you'll miss your plane."

Our luggage wheels spun fiercely behind us, our stilettos clicking rapidly along the way. That was the last time I wore stilettos for traveling! In the background we could hear the helpful young man yelling.

"Run, ladies! Run!" in his high-pitched, charming voice that started the giggles amongst us.

The whole way down the hall, we would glance at each other and burst into laughter as we ran. It slowed our progress significantly. With our stomachs in stitches, we did make it to our plane just as the girl was closing the door. I was a little disappointed as she let us in.

Secretly I would have loved to have been stuck in New York City for one more day.

***

The day of my accident, when it all happened -- when the money, the vacations, my dream of owning my first home, all combusted in the fire of destruction that galvanized into charcoal, the black ashes of my dreams and hopes all blowing away in the wind, leaving holes in my memory never to be rediscovered again -- for better or worse, is a day that will define me for the rest of my life.

Somehow the blow to my head made me forget how fun life could be. How happy I was to have a family; although not perfect, they were my family. I couldn't seem to find the bright and pleasant moments in things anymore; they seemed to be lost somehow amongst the new shadows that were forming in my mind, obscuring reality and mixing it in with the new non-world I found myself half trapped in. Life became hard, draining, and incredibly painful to live through, both physically and emotionally.

The laughter had stopped, and life wasn't fun anymore.

CHAPTER FOUR

The life of tranquility and serenity I once had, the ability to see good in all, seemed like a far-off dream. The new world of nightmares and chaos had taken over. Feeling as if I was separated from the human pack and no longer belonging in the human world, I found many monsters lurking in the dark corners. They seemed to snivel and sneer as they peered from the shadows with their razor-sharp teeth, setting their sights on the weak and wounded, waiting for the right moment to pounce. Pinned in a corner, I had only my claws for survival.

There seemed to be no end to the list of people who would prey on the defenceless. Perhaps they came from the new world, the new reality I was living in. Or perhaps my new reality made them visible, and I started to see people for who they really were.

My rationality was obscured and just as cloudy as the rest of my thoughts. Unable to make sense of the things I did remember, and forgetting everything else, I looked for answers. Before I realized it was my head causing all the mischief, I blamed others instead.

"I think she's keeping my money!"

"Who?"

"My agent!"

"Why?"

"I don't know, I just do."

With that thought in my head, I maneuvered and planned how to stop her from stealing from me. I lit a fuse and lost my agent.

I loved the feeling of being in front of the camera. There is something about performing that makes me come alive. A feeling of pure bliss ignites in me. My ego is set aside, and my characters come alive and fuel my inner desire to entertain.

I had been lucky to find my agent when I did. Especially after I had been out of the game as long as I had.

"There is a star quality in you that I can't teach," Dean Armstrong, my acting coach from the Armstrong Acting studios, confessed to me one day.

But with a young daughter to provide for, it was not practical to follow my dreams. Her desires and ambitions were all that mattered. However, when I found myself unemployed, it was a good way to make some extra cash.

How is it that we allow others to dictate our dreams, our future and our life? I often wonder, if I had parents who understood my artistic desires and stood by me, or a high school teacher to point me in the right direction, if I would have been able to make my dreams come true. There are far too many what ifs to count. But, I do have many more years to erase those 'what ifs' and turn them into action, followed by reality.

When the lights are out and the darkness is all that I see and feel around me, I dream before I dream my night-time's dreams. When there is no 'must do' or 'have to' I see a life filled with the desires I had as a child. The ones I believed would have come true if I had wished hard enough. That one day I would show the world, the villains of my life... see, see what I can do. I did it without you!

"If I'm honest, I have to tell you I still read fairy tales and I like them best of all." ~ Audrey Hepburn.

There was an older version of Cinderella that my eldest sister Cathy gave me as a young girl of seven. I remember it clearly to this day. Cinderella dropped a coin in the wishing well and was asked, "Would you prefer happiness now as a child, or when you grow older?"

She replied when she was older, because then it gave her something to look forward to. I agreed at the time.

Forget the fairy tales, I'm creating my own happy ending!

***

The difficult part of auditioning during the time of my recovery was the drive to Toronto. It was tiring and, with my head as it was, I had to find a way to make it work. I started driving down early, and resting prior to my auditions. I would calm myself with meditation and rest my head on the back of the car to stop the spinning and leaden feeling that would take over. If the role called for a positive me, I would think of all the wonderful things I could imagine. This created an inner glow that I felt through my eyes and would help mask the pain I was in.

In with the good air, out with the bad. In, out. In, out. *Thank you for my daughter and all the fun we have. In, out. Thank you for laughter. In, out. That I have a car to take me to auditions. In, out. Thank you for my shoes, oh how I like my shoes. In, out. Thank you for... keeping me alive.. really, am I happy about that?... shit, okay start again. In with the good air, out with the bad. In, out. Thank you for...*

After the audition for the First Choice Commercial, I was unsure of how I did. I kept going over the audition in my head again and again.

"I think I blew it!" I confessed to Maya.

"You always say that, then you get it."

"No this time, I think I really blew it!"

Darn, why didn't I smile more, or maybe if I wore the v-neck shirt. I can really use that money. Maya needs a new winter coat this year. Then when I didn't hear anything, I remembered that I said I wouldn't let them alter my hair. After all, it wasn't worth having to get a whole new set of photos if they made drastic changes. *Why did I say they couldn't alter my hair?*

My phone rang. I could see it was my agent's number. My skin started to tingle from the excitement. Could it be? Reaching for the phone, *no, calm yourself. She probably has another audition for you to go to, that's all.*

"Hi Maria!"

"You got the First Choice role!" my agent was eager to tell me.

"Really?" I was in utter shock.

The day before the commercial was shot, we had to go to a First Choice hairdresser to get our hair done. Everyone was getting highlights and cuts done. When they went to fully colour my hair, it was a different story.

"No, I'm sorry, you can't alter my hair!"

I could see the hairdresser and the executives looking at each other. As they pulled out my contract, they realized I did not agree to any alterations. I'm sure they kicked themselves for missing that.

"You look a lot younger than the audition tape and we needed someone a little more mature looking."

"I'm sure if you put the right kind of makeup on me, I can look older."

"We planned on colouring your hair."

"No, I'm sorry. Please feel free to call my agent."

"What about just some highlights?"

"No."

They talked amongst themselves for some time. The tension seemed to be rising, but I refused to budge.

"We'll do a California rinse that will strip your hair of some of the colour and products that are in it."

"That's fine."

As they were washing my hair, I could see the hairdresser's eyes light up. I normally straighten my hair, and this is how they saw it. However, it is naturally very curly. He called over the executives. They too seemed pleased.

They added product and styled my hair with my curls, instructing me to sleep in the bathtub that night with my hair not touching anything. Instead, I placed a pillow under my neck and let my curls hang over the edge.

I woke that morning excited. I love being in front of the camera. It's strange how much I love performing. I was incredibly shy growing up, but somehow if you put a camera in front of me or place me up on a stage, I light up and that fear melts away.

The day of filming, I sat in my car with my head in my hands to stop the spinning that built up during the two hour drive it took to get to Toronto from Cambridge. I did not want to put my head back against the head rest, for fear of flatting my curls. I reminded myself of all the things that made me happy. This routine always starts with my gratitude for my daughter. I wanted to truly believe in my happiness and to let it shine. After all, "the only international language is body language." This lasted half an hour, before the spinning slowed down enough to allow me to go in.

I sat in a chair as I got my makeup done and my hair touched up, watching some of the other actors being filmed, and reminding myself of everything I had to be grateful for, including shooting the commercial.

When it was my turn in front of the camera, I stood on a small, rotating stage, no more than a foot wide. Thank goodness for a small bar to hold onto, as the turning was not good for my head.

"We would like you to keep more of a straight face as you flip your hair up."

I stood on the platform and the light people did their thing and the camera man did his. The hair and makeup people kept touching me up. I can't remember about what, but we talked and laughed.

In the distance, I could see the executives watching in the monitors and again getting excited. The director walked up to me.

"Okay, we changed our minds. We want you to smile just like that and wink at the end."

I was happy to oblige. I am much more comfortable smiling than keeping a straight face.

The flipping of my hair, up then down, down then up, and the spinning of the platform was not a good thing. But the show must go on. By the end of it, my head was spinning like a spin-top toy I had as a child.

I can't tell you if it was the stress that caused the spinning, or the spinning that caused the stress, but my life was spinning out of control, and not in the right direction.

My ability to deal with the stress of events outside my control became my biggest enemy. My tool for dealing with stress was exercise. Perhaps it was the endorphins that released, but things always became clearer after a good workout or run. Yet after my accident, this was not the case.

I tried to explain to my doctor, "When I run, it makes everything go funny."

In my mind I was saying *When I run or exercise, it makes my head spin faster. My thoughts become more confused and my head feels as if it's going to explode with the swelling that develops.* Instead my thoughts stayed in my head and my voice remained silent.

My doctor instructed me, "Push yourself harder."

Although something told me I shouldn't, my doctor told me to. So push myself, I did.

With determination and persistence fueling me on, I glided fiercely through the streets. My body sang with the exertion. My blood pumped, my breathing was steady, and my stubborn pride ignited me. If willpower was enough, I would be victorious. I would not do any less than my forty-five minute run. I was determined to show my body what it was capable of.

Unfortunately, my thoughts became more and more jumbled. On top of losing my agent from my criss-crossed thoughts, I also lost friends, and I pulled away from my family. I can only hope that one day the people I was rude or unreasonable with will realize what I was going through and understand it was not me. Perhaps even forgive me.

As I ran, I could feel my head ballooning up. It felt as if it would explode. My thoughts kept getting more scrambled and my mind increasingly jammed up. Like a computer it started to slow down; then, as it became overloaded, it froze.

Maybe if I push myself past this pain, my head will just stop hurting and I'll be better.

I couldn't even touch my finger to my scalp without its sensitivity causing pain. However, if I was to push myself, that meant pushing myself through the pain. Even though I could no longer wear my glasses from the tightness caused by the swelling, I kept pushing myself on. Over and over again, day after day.

Mind over matter! It worked in the past, it will work this time too,

CHAPTER FIVE

Finding myself in a wilderness that I did not recognize was more than I could bear. I had my life and, although not perfect, it was perfectly lined up. It was mapped out and I was en route to achieving the American dream; that is, before I hit my detour. Heading down the new path, I had no map marking the best route to take, no bread crumbs to follow, and no lights to lead the way.

I now had to figure out how to survive with no income, an inability to process information, and a frightening lack of communication skills. Not to mention the inability to retain information crippling me, and any attempts to restore balance in my life.

The hardest part was struggling to get a hold of my faculties knowing my daughter and my family counted on me. But I continuously failed them, and this broke me even further. I felt as if I was being swept out to sea with no lifeboat to rescue me.

"I had an accident and a concussion." I would try to explain when I finally found my words. I hoped to get a helping hand. Instead, I got impatience and ignorance.

"I hit my head once and I'm fine, so you should be too." How can you explain something to someone who knows everything based on their own limited experience?

Try telling that to Natasha Richardson's family! I wanted to scream. People made me so angry. It was hard enough trying to explain what I was going through, let alone to knuckle heads of those who had no clue how to think past their own ego-driven thoughts and experiences.

As life started to crumble around me, I was grateful for my perfect credit and my savings. I had been preparing to purchase my first home and my first investment property. With no debt, a line of credit, and large savings, I was well set. I didn't worry too much when I was first laid off, as I thought it was only temporary. I was actually looking forward to a much-needed rest. Then I thought I would be called back to work. But as time went on, and I was not called back, I started to panic. I was lucky enough to get one small site, with a smaller competitor. But after quickly selling out of that community, I was once again on the lookout for work.

I can't even get a waitressing job. I don't know what I'm going to do. I would agonize as tears streamed down my face. I tried bitterly hard to figure out how to get a job, but the process of doing so amidst my cloudy mind and the painful thinking process at the time didn't bode well. I knew what I was once capable of, but those abilities were lost in the fog.

I felt as though I was living in a dark and empty room. A room that I was wandering around in aimlessly. My thoughts and memories were just out of reach and disappearing like a puff of smoke when I neared.

"Remember, we did that the other day," "Remember, you were there" or "I don't understand how you can forget something like that" were some of the questions directed towards me that would keep resurfacing.

Well I don't understand, how you can't understand... that I hit my FRIGGING head! You don't have to be Albert fucking Einstein to figure out the consequences of hitting my head!!! Stupid, stupid people!

Knowing that I should know something, or be able to do something that I couldn't, would unnerve, confuse, frighten, and piss me off all at the same time. The energy it would take just to get to a thought or a memory was excruciating. It was as if every road I went down in my memory had roadblocks, and I would go in circles trying to find my destination, getting turned around in the process and then forgetting what my original destination was. None of this helped me figure out how to live or earn an income.

"Mommy, you should write your stories."

Maya would encourage me to write, even before my accident. But it was never something I thought of as anything more than an activity to make Maya happy.

However, the fall seemed to knock the writer into me. I couldn't seem to stop writing or coming up with new plots and story lines on a daily basis. Perhaps it was the fact that it was all on paper and, even if I forgot what I had written, it was there to read and remind me. That pacified me and kept me going. It somehow seemed to calm and slow down the firing in my brain.

The first screenplay I wrote, I entered in the Canadian International Film Festival in Vancouver. But when a new idea popped in my head, I wrote my second screenplay in four days and submitted it with only an hour left to the deadline. The first script received honourable mention. The second was submitted without any edits or rewrites, and was a finalist. Later on, I converted that second script into a novel and it became one of the top thirty in a Hay House writing competition. I realized that perhaps I was on the right path.

I would sit at my computer and wouldn't stop. It was the only thing I could do that did not drain me of energy. I would write for ten or twenty minutes then rest, always looking forward to being able to start writing again.

Sitting in my room writing one night, I found myself wondering why Maya wasn't there. She normally came and sat by me and did her homework as I wrote. Feeling uneasy about not having her poke her head in, in the last little bit, was starting to concern me.

Maybe she's doing homework in her room. Getting up and walking was challenging. But, I saved whatever energy I could muster up for her and things she needed. I made sure she always got to school with a good breakfast and packed lunch.

Opening her door, I called out, "Maya!" Her room was empty.

My feet moved as rapidly as my heart was going at that moment. In and out of rooms, upstairs, downstairs, looking, searching, but not finding her. Panic started to grip me. *What if I forgot her somewhere and she couldn't call? What if she's in trouble and I can't figure out what to do to help her? Maya doesn't stay out wandering the streets. Did I forget her at ballet class or music? Shit, God please help me find her!*

Peering out at the dark night sky, I could feel my heart sinking. It wasn't like her to stay out like this and not tell me where she was.

I must have forgotten her someplace and I just can't remember. Panic gripped me. I hated myself, I hated my head, and I felt helpless.

Damn my fucking head!!! Figure it out, you have to. Please God, fix my head so that I can find her, please help me. Please, please. please! I begged.

Grabbing the phone list with all of Maya's friends' numbers off the fridge, I started to call them all one by one.

"Is Maya there?" I asked each time.

"No, I'm sorry, she's not," each person repeated one after the other, with my mind getting more jumbled and in danger of short circuiting. I wouldn't be surprised if smoke was coming out of my ears like in the cartoons.

My dad came home and found me pacing the hallway, walking in and out of Maya's room.

"What's wrong?" he asked with concern.

"We need to go find Maya!"

"What do you mean?"

"I can't find her!"

There it was, that look. He looked at me as if I was going crazy, trying to read me to see if I was serious. But I was serious, and he needed to realize it too, before something bad happened to his granddaughter.

"We dropped her off at Ashley's an hour ago," he stated, looking me dead straight in the eye "You came for the ride!" Ashley was a new friend, and her number had not made it up on the list yet.

Flashes of the ride over to her friend's house started to appear like a strobe light in my mind. In, out, and in circles, it repeatedly played, causing my head to spin, as if I was on the tilt a whirl at Canada's Wonderland, swirling up, down, and sideways.

"Oh ya, that's right. I guess I just forgot," I tried to play it off as if it wasn't a big deal.

Walking back to my room with lead feet, I slowly pulled back the blankets on my bed and slipped in between the crisp, cool cotton sheets. Resting my head on the soft, down-filled pillow seemed to be the only thing that made the world stop spinning long enough for me to catch my breath. Light-headed and queasy, I fell asleep, waking up with Maya beside me.

I was so confused at what was going on in my mind. I don't even think I own the ability to explain the fear that gripped me, not knowing if I would ever be right again. I was too ashamed and scared to let anyone know. I thought I was going crazy.

Looking up at Maya, I did what I did best. I hid my fears and emotions to protect her from feeling them, too.

"You need to make sure Ashley's number gets put up on the fridge."

"Okay."

Wrapping my arms around her waist, I fell back asleep as she watched a show on my TV.

The wilderness I was lost in would, on rare occasions, clear long enough for me to set my eyes on the sun's rays of clarity, only for it to disappear and leave me in darkness, trying to feel my way out again. The one ray of sun that was consistent was Maya. Even when I felt that disconnection from my feelings, my love for her was the only beacon of light that shone brightly enough to guide me back to me.

I managed to live through those years of darkness, for her.

CHAPTER SIX

I felt as if I was drowning in the vast sea, wave after wave crushing down on me, my body being dragged under. There was little time to breathe before the next towering wave rose above and broke crushing down, sending me spinning in a whirlwind fashion through its powerful momentum, reaching for the light, shining through the transparent surface of water just beyond my reach. I struggled to get to the surface and take a breath. The powerful weight of the water pulled with its mighty force and refused to release me from its grip.

Just as I thought I found solid ground and was finding my way back to recovery, the undertow would pull me back in.

I knew I was losing everything, I knew I was on the brink of one of the darkest times of my life. But I fought it with everything I had. In the end, everything I had just wasn't enough.

"How are you feeling?" My doctor would ask.

"Fine."

"Can you turn your head to the right?"

Oh no, he's asking me to turn my head again. Maybe if I go slow he won't notice the room spinning.

I could see a smirk on his face, but I could never figure out what it was for. Perhaps I was just imagining it. Now I realize how funny I must have looked, turning my head as slowly as I was. Although at the time I never could have understood that he could not see what was going on in my head, and he had no way of knowing how fast the room was spinning for me or that it was spinning at all. Therefore all he saw was a woman saying she was fine and comically turning her head at a snail's pace for no reason that he could fathom.

Leaving the doctor's office, I mistakenly thought that, if I was able to convince him I was okay, I was indeed okay. Tragically, I was far from it.

It was as if I was driving in the dark. Before the accident, I was accustomed to using my high beams so that I could see everything around me and make decisions based on all I saw. The state I was in after the accident was as if my high beams and my headlights were out and I was driving using a flashlight that flickered, and was duct-taped to the hood of my car. Trying to navigate through twists, turns and dead ends, with a small beam of flickering light. Thinking I could see, but missing everything I drove past.

I remember one day opening up Maya's closet door to find her crying in the corner. Watching the tears roll down her face, I stared at her, wondering what the hell she was doing. It annoyed me, watching her sniveling in the corner. I knew I had more patience for her, and that I was more loving before the accident, than I was feeling at that very moment. I tried to mimic the me before the accident to the best of my ability.

"What's wrong?" I asked.

She said nothing, but her lips annoyingly quivered.

"I'm not going to ask you again!" I demanded.

I didn't seem to be doing a good job at being the old me.

"I'm scared..." her tears flowed unrestrained, "...that I've lost you forever."

Feeling nothing close to sympathy, I did manage to realize that I once would have cared.

"Oh. Don't be silly, I'm right here." And I let her hug me.

Her arms clung around my neck and I realized that I was missing an awful lot. If I was missing how upset she was, what else was I missing? Things were so confusing and complicated. It seemed as if the pieces of life's puzzles didn't fit in my head anymore, and that some of the puzzle was misplaced.

***

When I was pregnant with Maya, I was only twenty-two and I was terrified of what being a mother was all about. I wanted to do it right. I grabbed every book I could get my hands on, including a book called *The Attachment Parenting Book: A Commonsense Guide to Understanding and Nurturing Your Baby* by Dr. William Sears and Martha Sears, RN. I learned that every child is different, and that what works for one doesn't necessarily work for another. But the most important lesson I learned from the Sears was to put the time in at the beginning. Most parents are too busy in the younger years of their child's life and then, when they became teenagers, they scramble to try and make a connection. The Sears taught me through their book that, if I made the time and put the effort into creating a loving relationship at the beginning, I would not have to try to make a connection with my teenage daughter, because one would already be there. They were right.

With that in mind, I always found time to play and connect. I even started to read to her when she was only months old, pointing at the words as I went along so that she would make a connection between the letters on the page and the words I was saying. I would leave the dishes or the laundry for the following day if I had to. I also learned from my older sister Cathy that the best time to get a child to open up was at night time, when the world and all its distractions had turned off. I would lie down beside her, playing with her hair, listening to anything she wanted or needed to tell me.

We would snuggle down and I would read to her. As she got older, we would take turns reading. The stories she seemed to like the most were the ones I made up using bits of information she provided for me. But it wasn't about the stories in the books, or the ones I told; it was about creating a safe place for her to be heard when she needed it, and a loving environment to show her how loved she was.

I also learned to decipher her tears. When I was in university and funds were limited, we had been walking past the toy section and a doll caught her eye. Maya, four at the time, remembered her lost doll that this one resembled. I told her she could play with it there, but had to put it back when we were done.

Pushing the doll in her pint-sized cart, she was quite content until it was time to put her back. Maya did not ask for the doll, she knew that what I said, I meant. Putting the doll back in its place, I could see one large crocodile tear roll down her chubby little cheek as she puckered up and gave the baby a kiss, and hugged her goodbye. My heart melted. Putting some of the groceries back, I let her purchase the doll. The look of surprise and joy on her little face was all I needed. Her happiness was a blessing to me.

Then the next time we were there, she found a stuffed puppy she wanted. Forcing fake tears, she looked at me as she hugged it. I smirked and shook my head no. She knew I wasn't buying into her act and that the dog would be staying in its place.

After the accident, I lost that knowing, the internal instinct and the ability to decipher her tears and her feelings. Unfortunately, this overflowed into all other areas of my life.

As time went on and I was able to start talking to my doctor and tell him what was going on, he sent me to a sports injury specialist who told me to stop everything. No more running, working out, or pushing myself. He told me what I knew was right, but needed permission to do. I needed to stop everything and just let my head heal. This seemed to help relieve some of the distress in my head, but not all of it. The fuzziness stayed, but the swelling, the severely jumbled thoughts and anger, seemed to subside a considerable amount.

The air never smelled better, the sun never felt warmer, and the sound of the birds was a beautiful song in my ears with a melody I could once again appreciate.

"I'm better."

The problem with this statement is that it can be taken in a couple of ways. It can be taken as "I am better" as in "I have healed fully" or "I am better" as in "I am better today than I was yesterday." The problem with a concussion is that people, including the patient, want to believe it's the former statement, that the post-concussion healing is done, ignoring the symptoms that are still lingering and focusing on the ones that have gone or subsided. Although I believe in focusing on the positive in most instances, when it comes to a concussion, this can be a tragic mistake.

With the world level again, I felt it was time to start to get my life back to what it was, and what better way than to go for a slow, leisurely run. I felt free again for the first couple days; I was no longer trapped in a body that was limited. I would run with the biggest grin on my face. Words can't describe how incredible I felt. To think that I once took my ability to run for granted. Never again. I was me again, or so I thought.

By the third day, it felt as if I had run straight into a brick wall at full speed. My head swelled, my mind was disorganized and convoluted more than it had been the past few months I had stopped exercising. Then there was the world spinning again at full speed. All my symptoms seemed to come back in full force. Only worse this time, because I had a taste of what life was like without the setbacks.

Tests revealed nothing; the neurosurgeon could only recommend that "I don't hit" my head again. *Great, I never would have thought of that!*

"Your symptoms are abnormal," she explained.

So you're saying I'm abnormal, that I'm different. Fine, give up on helping me, see if I care. The frustration was devastating. I thought if anyone, the top neurosurgeons in sports medicine could help me. But no; instead, when she couldn't figure it out, I felt she resorted to a well-practiced line. "It's abnormal."

The most perplexing was the word "abnormal" because the more I met and talked to fellow sufferers of head injuries, the more I realized how normal my symptoms were. Were we all abnormal, or were the doctors asking the wrong questions and giving up before they realized what the symptoms really were? The more I talk to those who suffer from what I was suffering from, the more I realize that four to five years to recover is typical, with symptoms still persisting. I realize that my inability to recall the amount of time that had passed, my mind unable to factor in the days after my accident, is something others suffered from too. The hideous spinning and confusion was just a new way of life that I hoped would go away one day.

"You'll either heal or you won't," was unfortunately the reality my doctor explained to me.

CHAPTER SEVEN

The tragedy that is called my life hit its peak. In a screenplay, this would be called the climax, when all seems lost to the character. The world they know crumbles around them, with no relief and no way out of the disaster they find themselves in. When the burden of saving the world they are in is resting on their shoulders. If they fail, all is lost to the world. I failed and, because of my failure, my family who counted on me, who I loved devotedly, lost everything.

This is my tragedy that will follow me in my broken heart forever. The harder I tried to make my brain work, to see clearly through the fog I was living in, to figure a way out of our situation, the more difficult it became to think and see things. When I needed my mind the most, it would short circuit and burn out. The spinning, the headaches, and the confusion still had not subsided, well over two years after my accident. Aside from not pushing myself, nothing gave me relief from my injury. Nothing seemed to set my head straight.

"I'm so sorry baby, but we have to leave our home, we just can't afford it anymore." The fear in her eyes was devastating, "It can't be helped! We'll have to stay with friends for now. Until I can figure something out."

The loss of our home was scary for everyone. We even had to find another home for our beloved dog Bailey and our loving cat Sylvester. I felt like a monster that should run off and hide in the darkness in shame. I let everyone who was counting on me down, especially Maya. Although she never saw it that way, I felt worthless. If it weren't for the love of my friends and family for taking us in, I don't know where we would have ended up. Couch surfing and relying on others became our new reality for the interim. *Is this a test?* I would ask in my prayers at night when everyone was asleep, *because I don't think I have the strength to pass it.*

In a spiral effect, I was whooshed from the easy comforts of a life I once enjoyed, to the broken land of 'lost and misfit toys' and broken dreams. The heaviness of my loss caused enormous pain, and I soon retreated from human contact. It wasn't hard to do, as people separate like the red sea when they sense failure. Not because they are bad people, but just because they know, if it happened to another, it could happen to them. Then, in an attempt to not be pulled down, they look the other way, pretending not to see.

Before my accident, I read an article on the importance of human eye contact and how important it is for someone to feel as if they belong to society. After this, I became acutely aware of society's habit of looking away when they see someone who just does not fit the 'perfect life'. A street person, someone with a deformity, or illness. I made it a point to go out of my way to look, smile and, when possible, to talk to these 'misfits' or beautiful souls, as I prefer to see them.

A short film I wrote and hope to soon produce came from two of these shiny souls, Alice and Wanda. When in university, I lived up the street from Alice. She had a limp as she dragged her right leg, and her right arm was always up in a tenser. But this isn't what Maya and I first noticed about her. Every time we saw her, she had the biggest and brightest smile. One that shined so bright, it was contagious. Just the thought of her makes me smile to this day.

"Hi!" she would bellow with a childish tone and a beaming grin that disguised her seventy-plus years.

Maya, then five years old, and I walked up to her and started to chat. This started a beautiful friendship. Alice had no friends or family nearby so, when we could, we would visit and bring her little treats. But it wasn't Alice who benefited from this relationship, it was us, from the warm feeling we always had after visiting her. I always found it so bewildering how someone with so little had so much to give.

Sometimes when I think of Alice, I wonder what happened in her life to get her to where she ended up. But then I realize, she found happiness even with the little she had.

Then there was Wanda. I was in Chicago, and I spent the day touring the city. When I saw Wanda on the streets begging for change, it pulled on my heart strings. She reminded me of Alice. Recalling the article and how important it is for someone to feel connected to society, I felt sad as I witnessed people walking past, not looking at her. Some gave money, some just kept going, but no one took the time to look at her, let alone smile. I was on my way to breakfast and I asked her if she would like to join me. She beamed and I could tell how proud she was to be able to walk into a restaurant as a customer. We had a lengthy conversation and, when it was time to go, I shook her hand firmly, looked her directly in the eyes, and said, "It was a real pleasure to meet you Wanda."

That is the first time I realized the immense 'power' of human contact. At first, she simply looked at my hand that was holding hers, with a bewildered expression. Then she slowly raised her eyes to look into mine. I could witness the transformation. After a brief period of confusion, her face lit up. Pride filled her eyes as she sat taller in her seat, and her smile radiated.

Could you imagine if all it would take to raise someone would be to see them and let them know that they too matter? That your soul sees their soul beyond worldly possessions and straight into the Being?

There I was after the accident, falling out of the land of the free to the land of the poor, bringing everyone down with me. If I had not had the accident, had worn a helmet or been more careful, our family would still be fully intact. I would have my career, our security and our home. We would be volunteering, and giving generously to charities, instead of receiving. How humiliating and crippling it is to find oneself in such a predicament.

***

Before I realized that I was not getting my job back, but after I had lost much of my savings and my life as I had once known it, I met Mark. He was kind and loving. I admired the way he spoke and cared for his children; he was someone I could respect. This was important to me. After our first date, I accepted a second. We were going to his farm to let our dogs run around. This is how the journey of my recovery began.

Following the directions I printed out from Google Maps, I got lost. It wasn't Google's fault. I couldn't find my way even with fluorescent arrows guiding my way. Especially after the accident, it was just how it was. I learned to give myself more time, knowing I would get lost. Finally pulling up to the address that matched the one on the paper, Bailey, sitting in the back, wagged his tail as he panted in anticipation. His large tongue was hanging out one side, and his adoring eyes were looking at me for a cue as to what he should do.

What the heck? This can't be right!

Looking at the large gates that announced the entrance to a grand estate, I was in shock. This was not the simple farm I was expecting.

I was feeling intimidated in my little Altima, with its one hubcap missing, idling in front of the iron gates. Rolling the window down, I reached for the pad and buzzed my arrival. Moments later, a familiar voice greeted me and the gates swung open.

The driveway was long and winding, lined with trees on either side. I drove past a large pond and up to the elaborate 'farm house'. Mark was standing there with his elegant doberman pinscher at his side. Maya's clumsy and overly-lovable lab jumped out of the car and ran about, smelling this thing and that. I didn't know what to think as he took me for a tour of his place. The indoor pool area, with a hot tub and steam room was larger than any hotel I have stayed at, and far more luxurious. The sitting room had a 26-foot fireplace, with marble and wood throughout. However, being a movie lover, I must say he had me at the elegant theatre room, adorned in royal blue with gold accents. Rows of leather seats and a screen larger than I've ever seen in a private residence were all very breathtaking.

As beautiful as his home was, it did little to impress me about the man himself. I was looking for happiness and a kind heart. He did have something going for him. In all that grandeur, he still seemed the sweet man that I had met just days before. I liked that he never gave himself away and that I had no idea of his success. That spoke volumes about his character.

Six months later, I was still smitten. I enjoyed his company, was learning about wine and fine dining. But dinners at home and walking the paths behind his home remained my favourite activity. On our walks, we would stop to feed the fish at the little white fence in front of his pond. It was peaceful and quiet, and I always enjoyed his company. One evening, he asked me what I would like to do. I felt like going out and dressing up in something other than my jeans and t-shirt.

I had just purchased a little Spanish-style black dress. I wanted to wear this for him, and Toronto wasn't too far off from his place.

"Let's go out to dinner and a show," I suggested.

"Do you have a passport?"

"Yes! Why?"

I soon found out. His private jet was waiting for us at the small airport near his home. As if that wasn't enough, he had the best surprise for me yet. One that I wouldn't have imagined in a million years. We once had a discussion on things we wanted to do, amongst them, race car driving, dog sledding, scuba diving and swimming with sharks. I wanted to fly a plane. His pilot presented me with my very own pilot log book. I was going to fly to New York City!

I can't believe he remembered; what a wonderful man! But as I sat there looking at the book, I started to worry. *How am I going to fly the plane for an hour and still have energy to go to the theatre?*

This was a bittersweet day for me. I wanted to enjoy every moment of that magical day, but I couldn't.

What am I going to do when my head starts spinning from fatigue? Looking at Mark, I wondered how I could tell this energetic and full of life man that I could barely go grocery shopping without having to rest my head, let alone fly his private jet plane. So I didn't.

Deciding to live in the moment, I was about to experience what it felt like to have a King Air jet in the power of my own two hands.

"Okay, you got this," the pilot looked at me once he had the plane lined up and ready for takeoff. I nearly fainted from panic. I could feel the blood drain and the palms of my hands dampen.

"Pardon?"

"You have to start somewhere."

I must have turned five different shades of white before I noticed the large grins on their faces.

"You're awful," I laughed.

The plane set off and started to lift. But with high winds, the little plane started to shake and rock. Gripping the seat tightly, I looked around at Mark to see if he was worried. They seemed to be laughing even harder at me.

"It's okay, this is normal!" Mark reassured me, and I let my grip loosen on the poor undeserving leather seat, just a little.

Up in the air, it was like a wonderful dream with white puffs of clouds under us. The view from the pilot's seat was incredible, the peaceful serenity of the open sky in front of us. When the pilot took it off autopilot and the plane was in my hands, it was incredible and frightening all at the same time. The palms of my hands were full of sweat and my heart fluttered. I panicked and let go.

"I can't do it!"

Justin the pilot laughed as he took over, "You can't make any mistakes, I'm right here. All you have to do is make sure these arrows stay in these lines. Or we'll be off our flight course and the navigation tower won't like it."

I was ready to try it again, and slowly I became comfortable and started to enjoy my lesson.

After landing, we found a car waiting for us to take us to our hotel. I liked the driver, he was funny and polite. However, it wouldn't be until the next day that I would be under his and Mark's persuasion. After the adventure I just had, I was unable to enjoy New York City as we walked around. I was feeling tired and fatigued. My head seemed to be swimming in fog, and it took everything in me to try and enjoy the wonderful day. Mark must have realized how quiet I was, and guessed what was wrong. He recommended we take a bike tour through Central Park. It was by far one of the best dates I had ever had, and there were still more to come. Although the date was enchanting, I spent much of the time worrying if I would feel too sick to go to the theatre and dinner that evening, as nausea was setting in from the spinning.

After taking a much-needed nap, the night went without a hitch. The show 'Jersey Boys' was amazing and well worth all the effort. However, after the show, dinner had to be cut short as I was unable to stay up and pretend that I was okay.

The next day, my head was clear. I always seemed to wake with clarity and energy. Lunch was a lot of fun. I remember chatting, joking, and getting to know each other even more. Back at the hotel, his friend had called.

"Tell him we eloped!" I laughed.

Mark found this amusing, and did as I said.

"He won't believe you!" I stated.

Mark smirked, "Oh yes he will!"

On the way to the airport, he talked about an investment opportunity he was presented with, and we continued with our little gag on his friend.

"Let's do it!" Mark smirked, "let's get married."

"But!"

"Why not?"

I didn't say a thing.

"I'll have the plane take us to Vegas."

I was stunned. Was my head playing tricks on me? I couldn't tell if he was still joking or if I was being proposed to. It had only been six months. My head started to spin and I couldn't seem to get my thoughts straight.

"He's talking oil investments, marry the guy!" The driver piped in.

I bit my lip and just stared. My thoughts were getting stuck in my head and mixing around. They got jammed and I couldn't respond. Not even jokingly, nothing was ever said on the subject again.

Sometimes I wonder what would have happened if I would have said "Yes."

CHAPTER EIGHT

Zipping, turning, winding at unthinkable speeds. Hugging the turns and accelerating at the straightaways. The revving of the engine, the smell of burning tires, and the feel of the race car's powerful engine in my grip was exhilarating beyond anything I have ever experienced.

The day was perfect. I got to drive a race car on a racetrack, all the while being instructed by a retired race car driver. What more can a girl ask for?!

"Do you want to go to the Bahamas with me?" Mark asked.

I just stared at him for a moment. It was such a long day already. My body and head were feeling the results of over-exertion. No matter how fun it was, I had pushed myself too far. Everything was just that much more cloudy. Then to have to think of an excuse, other than the truth of my limited funds, to explain why I couldn't go.

"I can't!"

"It won't cost you a thing. We'll take the jet and I rented a villa; a bunch of us are going."

The loom of exhaustion started to make me feel irritable, and my thoughts started to jumble up. All I wanted to do was rest and not have to think.

"It will be a lot of fun. We're entering a fishing competition; we can spend the day out on the sea."

What is he asking me to do? Oh yeah, Bahamas. Why can't he just understand that it's impossible for me, I have no money. I wish he would just stop!

My savings and credit lasted a couple of years, but didn't last long after that. Lucky for me, I found a small site to sell for a smaller builder. It was short-lived, but it helped. I could sell houses in my sleep, as it seemed to be second nature to me. When my head started feeling cloudy and heavy, I was able to rest on the couch and close my eyes in the model home to get the spinning to slow down.

"I don't think my boss will let me take the time off." I lied.

"We'll bring Richard and his girlfriend." Mark and my boss Richard had met before and hit it off.

How can I tell this man, who has absolutely no idea what money problems are, that I need my hourly wage to pay my rent? If I tell him, he'll just offer to pay it for me and that would be humiliating beyond belief. I couldn't bear it.

"No!" I said, and I turned away.

It was all too much, and my head was playing tricks on me again. My emotions were no longer in my control, they were under the power of the fog I was living in and he really started to piss me off. Not to mention my resentment to fate for playing such a cruel and unthinkable trick on me. There I was in a fairytale relationship, and I couldn't even enjoy all the things that would normally make me incredibly happy.

Before the accident, I would have been overflowing with joy and laughter. I would have gone home after my dates, jumped on the bed and sang all the wonderful things that had happened to Maya's delighted ears. She would have beamed with happiness and teased me jokingly, then she would have told me how happy she was that I had found someone.

Instead, it was painful and hard to bear the fact that I was unable to keep up to it all. That it all seemed laborious. Trying to be myself, the self before the accident, was next to impossible. The harder I tried, the harder it became.

As Mark continued to try and convince me to go to the beautiful Bahamas with him, I released his hand in frustration. I started to pull away from him both physically and emotionally.

We come from two different worlds, and he will never understand me. Or so I told myself.

My head refused to heal, and all the things that happened after my accident tore apart my life like a riptide.

That night and many more, my insomnia overpowered me. Noises seemed louder, and the slightest noise woke me. Restless and agitated, I got up in the middle of the night and slipped into the guest room to try and sleep. But the more tired I got, the more irritated and foggy I became.

Oh God, I just want to run away. Run away and hide where no one can find me. It wouldn't be so bad to curl up in a little ball and just let myself die! - But Maya, I can't leave her to fend for herself. To live her life alone in this miserable world. I have to keep trying for her. Trying to pretend like I am normal, like I am okay.

Mark went to a naturopathic doctor. I think he was a little upset, waking up and finding me gone. He told the doctor my symptoms and asked for advice. He came home later and surprised me with a bag full of supplements that she had recommended.

"Here, try this; it's good stuff and it will help you."

I didn't really have much faith in it. If doctors couldn't help me, how could a bag full of fish oil and other natural things help? But he seemed so pleased. To make him happy, I took it, regardless of my doubts. That night I took the California Poppy that the naturopathic doctor instructed me to take to help induce sleep. Not only did I have a full eight hours of solid sleep, it was the best sleep I had had in years. It was heaven sent!

Two weeks later, when I woke in the morning, I noticed something was different. The constant fog that I had been living in had lifted. Everything appeared crisper, my head seemed clearer and, for the first time, I felt like I was a part of this world again. I was no longer trapped in the in-between world I'd been living in. I couldn't believe how lucky I was to have my life starting to come back to me.

I healed more in two weeks than I had in two and a half years, just from a bag of supplements. *How can this be; how come no one told me this before?* The joy I felt at knowing that there was a possibility, that I could be me again, overwhelmed me with happiness.

Wow, our bodies are so incredibly smart. All we have to do is give them what they need and they will heal themselves. I continued to ask myself, *If these supplements can have such an incredible impact on me, what else can I give my body to continue to heal itself?*

No longer feeling alone, I felt as if someone was watching over me and guiding me. I started to wonder what other miracles were in store for me.

Continuing my research, I read medical journals, health books, and blogs to discover what our bodies need, discarding everything I thought I knew about health until that point and using only common sense and simplicity as my guide. I realized, no matter how complex our body is, it really is very simple. We are made up of billions of cells and molecules that are all made up of the same thing.

Then I had a eureka moment. If we give our body what it needs, not only will it heal what we are trying to heal, it will heal our whole body; after all, our cells make up every part of us.

Weeding out all the fads of the moment and staying away from all the false promises that "this one pill" or "this one thing" is all you need, I learned that it was a multitude of nutritious foods, supplements, our thought process, and the quietness of meditation that our body uses to be the healthiest version of itself.

Then one day I noticed that, even though I was still not able to exercise, I was back down to my high school size. That was five dress sizes smaller than what I was just prior to the accident, when I was taking two dance classes a week, working out, running every day, and eating what I had thought was a healthy diet. I couldn't believe how an organic, non-chemical diet could heal my body in more ways than one. Aches and pains I lived with for years, that just became a part of life, disappeared like magic. Those that noticed and followed what I was doing received the amazing benefits that I had stumbled across, all because of one bag of supplements.

However, as I continued to heal, I found the one thing I still could not do was let my blood elevate. Every time it did, regardless if it was exercise or stress, my symptoms came back. I went back to the neurosurgeon.

I found the tests frustrating because I knew I should be able to do them; they were the types of tests I always accelerated at. Yet I couldn't figure out the simplest of the puzzles.

"It's time to try to challenge your mind. Build it back up like a muscle. Take a college course or something similar, but not one with an exam. That will be too much for you."

The idea of painting hit me. I had never found the time to paint the portraits of Maya that I wanted, so I thought this would be a perfect opportunity, as I found myself still without a job, and time to do it.

"Can I paint?" I asked.

"That would be perfect. As long as it's not a Picasso," she warned jokingly.

Excited to get home and paint, I pulled out some of the pictures I had taken at Mark's cottage in Muskoka. I found one that I loved. We were on the boat and he stopped so that I could take some photos of a little rock island with a couple of beautiful trees and flocks of birds. I wanted to start small and work my way up to the portrait of Maya. I was also excited as I wanted to make it a gift to him for starting me on the path of recovery.

But as I started to put paint to canvas, it wasn't long before my head shorted out and started to spin again. I realized that even this I could not do. *How is it that I can no longer paint, but I can write like there is no tomorrow? It doesn't make any sense that I somehow lost one talent and then gained another.*

I kept trying, but I just kept getting infuriated at not being able to paint a simple landscape. I decided to slap some paint on canvases anyway, and they turned out more like a child's finger paintings. I cried for the lost talent that I once loved.

If it wasn't for my newfound ability to write, I think I would have died a little more inside. Creativity is a part of me; it defines me.

Once again, I stopped everything. I stopped trying to run, to push my mind and to find myself again. My life continued to spiral down and I started to wonder if I would ever be completely me again. Many attempts at restoring my ability to run resulted in my head feeling like it would explode, and my thoughts cluttering, my emotions heightening, and losing more people I cared about. I gave up. If it was a choice between my mind and getting back my old drive and abilities, I chose my mind and the ability to think clearly.

Continuing to eat healthy and take my supplements, I continued to improve. Every half year or so, I would realize that I could do more, think more, and just had that much more energy. I even worked my way up from a five-minute walk to a forty-five minute hike without feeling dizzy.

I decided to be grateful for the ability to walk and to think, and I didn't look back again.

CHAPTER NINE

'...while freedom is a gift from God, it must be secured by His people here on Earth.' ~ President Barack Obama

As my life started to repair and my head started to heal, my soul too became full of love. I could feel sympathy, caring, sorrow, and pain for others once again. Sadness would occasionally creep in as my empathy would overwhelm me. Perhaps making up for lost time. Every good deed I witnessed, a commercial or a movie, sent me into tears.

Then one day, although I can't recall exactly what it was that hurt me, I remember feeling sad for the unkindness I witnessed around me, how cruel people could be. I couldn't understand how anyone could purposely set out to hurt another. I thought of all the people who took advantage of me while I was struggling with my injury, in work and out of work. I thought of all the unjust and bad things that happened after the accident, when I could not properly take care of myself.

The day was January 21, 2013. President Barack Obama's second inaugural speech was on the television.

'We recall that what binds this nation together is not the colors of our skin or the tenets of our faith, or the origins of our names. What makes us exceptional -- what makes us American -- is our allegiance to an idea articulated in a declaration made more than two centuries ago: "We hold these truths to be self-evident, that all men are created equal; that they are endowed by their Creator with certain unalienable rights; that among these are life, liberty, and the pursuit of happiness."

These words, at a time that I was feeling overwhelming sorrow for mankind, hit like a magic wand. I started to weep tears of joy, love, and hope. It was only just over 150 years ago when slavery was a part of the American way, but thank God not anymore. If in such a short time we, the world, could bear witness to a president of darker skin in the United States, then there was hope for humanity. Hope that, perhaps one day in less time, we as people could witness world peace, world freedom, and a world where we realize that banning together in love and harmony can create the life we all dream of. A colour-blind, gender-blind world, tolerant of each other and each other's beliefs.

As more tears ran freely down my face, I fell to my knees in gratitude. I had just realized that I could feel again! I could love, I could care, and my heart was once again intact and free to feel love, sorrow, and kindness for others.

I'm me again!

***

After I realized how much my diet and thought process affected my health and mind, I couldn't get enough of healthy eating and positive thinking, and I kept getting better. The fogginess and the clouds all seemed to lift. However, there was still one obstacle to overcome. No matter how much I improved, I still was unable to work out or allow my blood pressure to rise. It would continue to set me back. I couldn't move on with my life, because I knew that at any moment I could have a setback and ruin any advancement I had made. I didn't want to find positive opportunities, as I feared what would happen if something happened to my head again.

I was getting tired of explaining my head injury and how it was affecting my life, especially after I was asked how long it had been. The response was always the same. "Really, over four years." How does one put a time limit on the healing recovery of a head injury? You can't. Each injury is as unique to the individual as a fingerprint.

Then I remembered. The mind is a powerful thing. I knew this before the accident and somehow lost sight of it. But now that I had my mind back, it was time to use it to its full potential. I started visualizing being fully intact again, running, exercising, and dancing my way back to a healthy mind and body.

Visualizing does many things. It helps you believe in yourself enough to take the necessary steps to achieve your desired goal, thus helping others to believe in you. 'Body language is the only international language'. Regardless of whether or not people are aware of it, they are indeed responding to the non-verbal communications you are sending. The most important thing is that you are also responding to your feelings and how others treat you.

I had no idea how I would overcome my final hurdle to self healing, but I knew I would do it.

A friend of mine, who also has an incredible story on his mission to find health for others, was having a book-launching party for his new book *Ikkuma: The Evolution of Vitality*. On my way into the building, I struck up a conversation with a man on health. Later on, he found his way into the launch party and we discussed health and the importance of nutrition. I then confessed that I was the size I was not due to fitness, but a healthy diet. After hearing why I was no longer able to allow my blood pressure to elevate with exercise or any mental activity that caused too much stress, he told me his story and how he too had the same problem.

"It's not in the head, it's in the back and neck... I started to go to a Facial Stretch Therapist (FST). He realigned my spine and, after a few appointments I was fine," he explained.

It's funny how things happen sometimes. For the past few years, my sister Mary-Jo had been studying FST and in fact had advanced to an instructor. We had discussed my visiting and having her stretch me, but we always ended up doing other things. Had I known what would follow after one session with her, I would have made it a priority to have her stretch me.
Days later, I made my way down to her and she went to work on realigning me.

"You're hyper flexible, just like me." I looked at her strangely, not knowing what she meant. "We're more flexible than we should be. Most people can't bend this way. I'm not sure what I can do for you."

As flexible as I was, it still felt amazing. She lifted my feet and swung them back and forth gently. She took my legs and wrapped me around like a pretzel. I could feel my muscles all relax; it was better than a massage.

She made her way up to my neck area, "Oh wow! Are you kidding me, what the hell did you do to your neck? This is bad!"

Mary started to move my neck and head around. It was tender and sore, but I could feel it working. Then I started to laugh "Are you really pulling my hair?" She just smiled and kept tugging my hair, and I could feel my spine straighten and stretch.

Then it happened! I felt a pop on the right side of my neck and a pop on the right side of my spinal cord half way down my back. Visions of being on the hill in Blue Mountain and falling popped into my head. I fought the tears, trying to keep my sister from sensing the emotional breakdown I was fighting not to have. Then all of a sudden, I felt an adjustment in my inner right ear, the one that gave me so much trouble.

What is going on? This is insane! How could this fix my hearing? Oh my God, don't cry!

Don't cry! Could this be it; could this have been all I needed to fix the rest of my problems? The last piece of the puzzle.

I wanted to believe, I wanted to put on my running shoes and just run! But I was scared. *What if it doesn't work? What if I try to exercise and it happens again? The stupid spinning and fuzziness, I don't think I can take if it doesn't work.*

I stopped those thoughts and replaced them with belief in my sister, belief in myself and my healing. I started small; it had been over four years since I'd been able to work out. I didn't want to push my body too far. I put in DVDs of workouts, and each day I did a little more. Each day that I didn't revert back to the wacky messed-up head, I became more confident. I pushed myself harder, I pushed myself farther and, just like that, I was me again! I could work out, I could hear normally, and I felt great! A few more reflexology appointments with my baby sister, and the next goal is running again.

There really is no limit to what we can do when we believe in something and pursue it with relentless determination.

Life is a lot like water drifting through our life.
We can either focus on a destination and fight the tide,
or we can enjoy simply being in the water
and allow it to take us someplace new.
Someplace perhaps far greater,
then we could have ever dreamed for ourselves.

Part Two

Everything to Give

HEALING FROM POST CONCUSSION SYNDROME

It took years for me to heal and, in fact, as I sit here writing this, it has been five years eleven days, and there are still memories lost, and healing to be done. Yet I feel a tremendous joy for the healing that I have experienced. However, I also feel an overwhelming sadness for all of those who still suffer and are lost in the fog I once was in. A head injury is not something you can rush to heal from; however, there are actions you can take to help in the process.

I heard of a young teenage girl who suffered a head injury the same way I got mine, skiing. She can't go to school dances, and has to sit in a room by herself instead of going to her classes with her friends. She sits in her room alone with headphones on because everyday noise is intolerable. I was informed of a man who, after being mugged and hit in the head years ago, still suffers and is not the same. A young boy who was involved in a car accident. I even spoke with someone who after eleven years still suffers headaches and outbursts in personality. Another who told me it took over four years to get his life back. These stories both helped me understand that I was not alone, but also painedme for I knew how they suffered.

For those who are still lost in the fog, suffering from their head injuries and feeling alone, I tell you now, I am here with you always. In my heart, in my thoughts and in my prayers. For you

I provide the following list of supplements I took to help me heal faster in two weeks than I had in two and a half years. I call the list my Concussion First Aid Kit, I hope it has the same impact on your recovery as it did on mine.

My Concussion First Aid Kit

- Carlson Cod Liver Oil, 1000 mg: one in the morning and one at night
- Ion-Mag (premium ionic magnesium with full-spectrum trace minerals) drops: 10 drops in the morning and 10 at night.
- PhosChol Polyenylphosphatidylchoine PPC 900 mg/capsule: two in the morning and two at night.
- Enteri Phyte California Poppy: one at nighttime to induce sleep. (Unlike pharmaceutical sleep aids, the California Poppy left me feeling awake and refreshed with no side effects eight hours after taking)

The above was prescribed to me by a naturopathic doctor. Please consult with a natural path doctor for your dose amount.

I was instructed by a naturopathic doctor that it would take months before I felt any results from the above supplements. The fact that I felt a positive change in two weeks was incredible. However, it might take you longer, as there are many different factors that can contribute to the amount of recovery time for each individual. Remember each head injury is as unique as your fingerprint.

It's also very important, when you are dealing with a head injury, that you avoid alcohol, stress, and physically demanding activities. As hard as it is when you are still experiencing symptoms, be honest with yourself and don't push harder than you know you should. Let your brain heal before you try to go back to your old routine. After all, your brain controls everything you think, say, and do. It's the hard drive of the human body.

> "Carefully watch your thoughts, for they become your words. Manage and watch your words, for they will become your actions. Consider and judge your actions, for they have become your habits. Acknowlage and watch your habits, for they shall become your values. Understand and embrace your values, for they become your destiny."
>
> - Mahatma Gandhi

RELAXING THE MIND AND BODY

Some people may remain in a constant state of tension and anxiety for their future, past and present. Not realizing that living in the moment is all that really excises. Living for each breath, each hug and each new memory means truly finding the peace in each perfect second that accumulates to create our life.

It's as simple as finding the time to stop and take a deep breath in, and remembering to thank the plants and trees, that generously give the oxygen we breathe. Then showing them our gratitude by exhaling. Our relationship with plants is a balance of give and take, as all healthy relationships are. Including the relationship you hold with yourself.

At times it could be our own thoughts that cause irrational behaviours and beliefs that might be hindering our ability to find health and happiness. Finding the blessings hidden in every situation helps you learn how to master your thoughts, to find the truths that are sometimes hidden beneath what may appear as a setback. When in reality it is only something being removed from your life that no longer serves you. It's removed to make room for something new and better. It's not always easy to see but, when one learns to find those hidden blessings, it becomes more and more apparent.

In a world of constant mental stimulation, its also important to remember to take a moment to quiet the mind; make still the thoughts that clutter your energy. Working with your inner Being to achieve this can be rewarding beyond anything you can imagine. To find a peace within yourself is a true gift that should be desired by all. Living in harmony with yourself is the most precious gift you can give to the world.

This can be a difficult task to master; however, one method that can be used to start the process is the acquiring of happy thoughts. It can alter the brain with its extreme plasticity, to become more positive in its perceptions of events. To aid in the process I encourage you to create a 'little happy book'.

To do this, get a little journal that fits into your pocket or purse. Make sure the colour makes you feel happy every time you look at it. In this little happy book write down a list of things that make you happy and that you are truly grateful for. Carry it with you everywhere. Every time you encounter a true intrinsic moment of joy, jot it down. Any time you're feeling down or just heavy in negative and self-damaging thoughts, pull the book out. Pick something from your list of happy thoughts and concentrate on it. Think about why it makes you happy, be grateful for it and really concentrate on feeling the blessedness it brings to you. Keep doing it until you can feel the corners of your mouth turn up. When you're done reflecting and the thought of what was bothering you comes up, recite these words.. "This too shall pass" (*The Secret* by Ronda Byrne) and let it go. Move past that awful feeling of heaviness and embrace the light and loving feelings your happy thoughts gift you with.

When you start to master your feelings and thoughts, it's time to master what you say and how you say it. When you find you're reciting negative words, find a way to reverse what you're stating into a positive light. Your thoughts and words will be what defines you to yourself and to others, because they will determine how you act.

As you master these first steps you'll slowly sense your body relaxing. The tightness will start to loosen its grip, simply by your training your mind to be happy. This is when the real magic begins because, once your thoughts alter and your body unwinds and you start to act in a happy way, you will find more joy.

Everyone you encounter is brought into your life for a reason. Be fully aware of this and, with each person that comes and goes from your life, ask 'What is it that I am to learn'? Being mindful of this can help bring a fuller understanding and tolerance for all situations, regardless of the degree of perceived negative or positive influence they bring to your life. However, nothing need be negative, if looked upon from the perception that all life's lessons are bringing you to a fuller awareness of yourself.

Next, stop taking yourself seriously and go out and have some FUN! Sometimes we put our heads down and plow through life, working long hours and not taking a break until we reach our projected target or goal. But the problem is, once there, we tend to set even loftier targets and goals. However, you will find that, if you take a break once a week, put it all away and go out to have some pure blissful fun, you will actually accomplish more, and with much more efficiency. Your mind and body will be able to relax and recharge, much like hitting the reset on your computer or pulling out the battery in your cell phone, it just gives us the necessary reboot. Or you can keep going at that workaholic pace until you get sick, leaving you no choice but to take a much longer break; because your body is so exhausted, it forces you to stop.

This is a BIG one. Let yourself feel the bliss! When you are happy, feel it and don't shy away from it. Forget about being that nonchalant guy or gal, pretending it's not that big of a deal. Every moment of happiness is a gift that should be treasured and yelled from the roof top. Don't be afraid of what other people think; just live and feel every ounce of your joy. If people look at you funny, just remember this ... 41% of Americans were against President Obama, yet he still became the President of the USA. Be the President of your own life and stop trying to make everyone else happy. It's about making yourself happy! Then surround yourself with other like-minded, positive and happy people.

Do you remember the Tom Cruise incident where he jumped up and down on Oprah Winfrey's couch? I look at that incident a lot differently than those people who criticized his exuberant display of joy. They disapproved and called him 'crazy', as if just by saying the word it made it true. (Just because someone says something doesn't make it so!) I believe those people are afraid to let themselves feel or express joy or happiness in their own lives, so they can't handle seeing others who are overjoyed with happiness. It makes them feel uncomfortable because they don't understand it; they live in such an unhappy and staid state themselves. It makes them feel better when they sling insults and disapproval, in an attempt to bring people like Tom Cruise down to their level of sedate unadventurous living.

Instead, I say reach for the sky when it comes to feeling overjoyed with love and happiness. Try to bring yourself up to Tom Cruise's level of happiness. Jump on couches, jump up and down on your bed. Remember how good that felt when you were a kid? If you can't bring yourself to do that, then jump up and down on the neighbour's trampoline. I like to put 'Kiss' by Prince on and hop up on my coffee table, close my eyes and just *dance*. Whatever you do, stop holding back and 'Express Your Happiness'!

There will be times when people do hurtful things that affect you. You can't help that, but what you can control is how you respond. Both in mind and action. Don't let it take over your life in a negative way. If someone wrongs you and you let it fester, knot your stomach, and let your mind race with anger or worry, that is only going to affect you. Ask yourself what lesson you can learn from that situation and then try forgiving the person. I'm a strong believer that, when people are acting in unkind and hurtful ways, it's because they are hurting within themselves, and they are in need of kindness and compassion. You do not have to agree with their actions, but you have to remember their behaviour is a reflection on them, not you. This is a hard one to master. However, you will feel lighter and healthier if you can accomplish letting go and forgiving.

With that said, remember you do not have to keep submitting yourself to unhealthy or negative situations. Forgive the people who may have hurt you, then let them go from your life with love. Try to surround yourself with like-minded individuals. That can be both in healthy eating as well as healthy attitude and behaviours. By surrounding yourself with positive influences, you will create an environment in which you have no choice but to succeed in becoming the healthiest and happiest version of yourself possible.

THE BRAIN AND SLEEP

Sleep is vital for optimal brain function.

Beauty sleep is putting it mildly. Sleep not only helps with a healthy fresh glow, it helps your brain become beautiful too. Without realizing it, you could be taking your brain for granted, pushing it too hard and just not appreciating it for all its wonderful complexities. I LOVE and adore my brain and, although I am grateful I no longer need to sleep twenty hours a day as I did after my accident, I make sure to give my brain all the sleep it needs. I know it's common to brag about how little sleep you can go on nowadays; heck, I did it too before my accident. Now I realize the ludacrisy in it. Lack of sleep ages your brain, slows its function and distorts its memory.

Our brains get a lot of information throughout the day. Think of it like folders or files; we need to get the right amount of sleep so that our brains can file everything away in its proper place. If you don't get enough sleep, your brain will not be able to store everything before you wake up and the information will get lost and/or misplaced.

> *When people learn something and then are tested the next day, their performance is often better the second day than the first, but only if they sleep adequately during the night.*
>
> (Stickgold, James, & Hobson, 2000: Stickgold, Whidbee, Schirmer, Patel, & Hobson, 2000)

> *The first thing experts will tell you about sleep is that there is no "magic number." Not only do different age groups need different amounts of sleep, but sleep needs are also individual. Just like any other characteristics you are born with, the amount of sleep you need to function best may be different for you than for someone who is of the same age and gender. While you may be at your absolute best sleeping seven hours a night, someone else may clearly need nine hours to have a happy, productive life.*
>
> www.sleepfoundation.org

Here is a sleep Chart; however, remember this is a guideline. There is no "magic number" as we all vary in our optimal sleep level.

Age	**Sleep Needs**
Newborns (0-2 months)	12-18 hours
Infants (3-11 months)	14-15 hours
Toddlers (1-3 years)	12-14 hours
Preschoolers (3-5 years)	11-13 hours
School-age children (5-10 yrs)	10-11 hours
Teens (10-17 years)	8.5-9.25 hours
Adults	7-9 hours

www.sleeptracker.com

Dr. Daniel Amen, who wrote the book *Use your Brain to Change Your Age* explains that, not only does your brain need sleep in order to properly function and to be at its prime, a lack of sleep can prematurely age your brain. He also states that "Brain injuries matter, they damage the brain... One head injury can ruin a life." I second that. Please, please use a helmet when participating in any sport that requires it, no matter how proficient you are. I put my first pair of skis on when I was five years old, yet after 20 years of skiing I had an accident. It can happen to anyone, anytime.

"After all your brain determines how you think, how you feel, how you act, and how well you get along with other people. Your brain even determines the kind of person you are. It determines how thoughtful you are, how polite or how rude you are. It determines how well you think on your feet, and it is involved with how well you do at work and with your family. Your brain also influences your emotional well being." ~ Dr. Daniel Amen

Dr. Amen shows how injury, lack of sleep, bad food and unhealthy choices can affect your brain function and, in essence, who you are as a person. Take young children that are in need of sleep. They become irritable, fussy, and temperamental. As adults, we might learn to mask these behaviours slightly, but we still feel the same effect as a child would.

Think about the last time you got a good night's sleep and how great you felt the next day. Why not try to accomplish this every night? That way you wake up feeling alert, every day. You'll feel calmer, relaxed, sharper and balanced throughout your waking hours.

But what happens when you can't sleep? Throw in a head injury and you have a major problem. Sleep plays an important role in your brain's plasticity, your mood and your cognitive processing. In a brain that is trying to recover, sleep deprivation can hinder the recovery and exacerbate the symptoms.

"Traumatic brain injury (TBI) can result in both short- and long-term physical, cognitive and neurobehavioral impairments for survivors. These impairments can result in devastating personal and societal consequences, impacting return to the community and pre-injury lifestyle. Complaints of disturbed sleep, excessive daytime sleepiness and disorders of arousal have been well-established as being among the most pervasive, enduring and common sequelae of TBI. Sleep/wake disturbances are prevalent across all levels of severity and across the continuum of recovery, often evolving over time. This is critical from the perspective of recovery from TBI, as adequate sleep is essential for general healthy functioning even in a normative population. Recent studies of healthy adults reveal that, following days of chronically restricted sleep of duration below 7 hours per night, significant daytime cognitive dysfunction accumulates including lapses of attention, slowed working memory, reduced cognitive processing, depressed mood and preservation of thought - sleep restriction produces unhealthy physiological consequences. Furthermore, sleep plays a crucial role in neuro-synaptic plasticity and neurogenesis. However, up to 70% of TBI survivors report symptoms of insomnia including difficulty falling asleep, staying asleep, sleep fragmentation and difficulties with early wakening, across the continuum of recovery." - (http://informahealthcare.com/bij ISSN: 0269-9052 (print) 1362-301X (electronic) Brain Injury - Evaluating the impact of treatment for sleep/wake disorders on recovery of cognition and communication in adults with chronic TBI)

www.sleepfoundation.org

When you have a head injury, a good night's sleep becomes essential. A major factor of suffering a concussion is the continuous pain one can find oneself in. Headaches, back pains, and disturbed sleep can create a victim of an endless cycle. "Sleep and pain are also inter-related with anxiety and depression. In Fact, insomnia, anxiety or depression are frequent co-morbidities associated with chronic pain. Disrupted sleep and rest patterns and poor sleep quality were positively correlated with depression and pain-related disability. The outcome is = reduced quality of sleep. Obviously it can lead to non-restorative sleep. Same thing with brain injury or pain; it affects some of these stages and this results in a decrease in total REM sleep or deep sleep and = no recovery." states Guy Chamberland, M.Sc., Ph.D., Master Herbalist, who is a health product consultant and performs clinical research on herbal therapies and chronic conditions, such as anxiety, insomnia, and pain.

Even though I was sleeping about twenty hours a day the first year or so after my accident, and as it slowly decreased in hours, I was not getting what Dr. Chamberland calls 'Restorative Sleep'. He also points out the "inter-relation of pain with sleep! It is a bidirectional relationship where poor sleep enhances pain and enhanced pain further disturbs sleep." Chamberland further states that "Sleep has an essential function especially for recovery."

Brain injuries can significantly affect the quality and quantity of sleep, thus slowing down and hindering recovery. With a heightened sensitivity to stimuli and in many cases a acute sense of hearing, a night of constant wake/sleep pattern is inevitable. Furthermore, it can affect your day and put you in risk of further accidents, as inadequate sleep is a major cause of accidents. It has a similar effect to using drugs and alcohol.

Before my accident a bad night's sleep led to a decrease in my ability to function for the following day. However, after my accident, a poor night's sleep leads to an inability to function at all. When my sleep is interrupted for just one night, I can lose anywhere from one to three days. I regress back to the fogginess and slowed cognitive functioning.

Even now with my recovery at an all-time high, I am reminded of how important the role of Enteri Phyte California Poppy (the sleep aid in My Concussion First Aid Kit, pg 84) is in my life. There are times when I forget to monitor myself and I overdo it. I can become overanxious or excited and disturb my sleep just like anyone else. However, unlike others, the lack of sleep hinders the continuous progress I am making in my recovery. This is when the California Poppy is crucial to my ability to regain balance with a proper sleep pattern.

"With many health conditions, restful sleep is the best remedy the body needs in order to recover. California Poppy is one of the best remedies because it provides a calming restorative sleep. Research has shown that quality sleep alone is pivotal for recovery from injury." explains Guy Chamberland.

At some point after my accident, I do recall taking a sleep aid that my doctor prescribed. It left me feeling drowsy and nauseous the next day. I did not feel rested at all and I stopped taking it as it hindered my day. However, after taking Enteri Phyte California Poppy, I had the first full night's sleep that left me feeling rested after my accident. It was amazing. I knew I had hit a proper sleep cycle, especially after I sat up in bed and reflected back on the crazy dreams I had had the night before.

Ikkuma Evolution of Vitality Sleep Tips:

- Try to **maintain your circadian rhythm.** Constantly changing your sleep patterns confuses your body. The orchestra gets out of synch.
- **Avoid bright lights at night.** They can suppress melatonin for up to 90 minutes after they have been shut off. Dim the lights and avoid TV.
- **Black out your bedroom.** Even small amounts of light can disrupt your production of melatonin and serotonin, affecting sleep and mood.
- **Eliminate noise.** If you live in a noisy neighborhood wear earplugs. This includes mental noise. Try to have a calm and peaceful environment.
- **Avoid late night caffeine**, as it can disrupt your sleep. However, even midday caffeine can affect you. http://bit.ly/10lkggp
- **Skip long daytime naps.** Your circadian rhythm can be shortchanged by long naps. Stick to 15-25 minute naps to get a boost.
- **Deal with chronic stress.** It affects every part of your health including sleep. Anxiety can promote adrenaline and cortisol production.
- **Steer clear of artificial sleep aids.** The sleep aid market is booming despite showing marginal improvements. http://bit.ly/YQXtuH.

The last post in the box above from Ikkuma might look as if it contradicts everything I have said about Enteri Phyte California Poppy. However, it does not in any way. I agree one hundred percent with Gary LeBlanc on this point. Stay clear of artificial pharmaceutical sleep aids. They only made me feel worse. However, California Poppy is a non addictive, plant base sleep aid that works without any side effects to date. I am a strong believer in natural healing, and I found that the California Poppy worked with my body to help restore it to its natural sleep rhythm. In fact, after California Poppy helped me get all the restorative and body healing sleep I needed after my accident, I find I do not have to take it on a regular basis. In fact, unless I am feeling stressed or some factor out of my control affects my sleep cycle I don't need it anymore. I still take it, but only when my mind is racing, I've had an overly taxing day, or I haven't had a good night's sleep and I am unable to find that natural sleep pattern on my own. When I take California Poppy now, I find it gives my body the needed assistance to put me back on track. My body then takes over and I am back to a natural night's sleep without any aid. The natural plant-based formula truly has been a life saver for me and I know, without it and all the supplements in my Concussion First Aid Kit, I wouldn't be where I am today on my journey to recovery.

MIND AND BODY CONNECTION

"There is plenty of evidence that meditation can improve a host of issues, such as pain and cognitive function, and anxiety is perhaps at the top of the list," explained lead author Fadel Zeidan, PhD, a postdoctoral research fellow in neurobiology and anatomy at Wake Forest School of Medicine, in Winston-Salem, North Carolina.

While at university I learned of a study that was started due to an observation made at a mental health facility. At the hospital, doctors noticed that the patients destroyed paintings with manmade structures and left fully intact those that only represented nature. This was then repeated under observation at several other facilities. It is believed that cities have a high population of mental illness not because they attract mentally ill individuals, but because they create them.

Our minds are not created to withstand constant stimulation. There is good news though. You don't have to move out of the city if you don't want to. There is a way to find the calm and peace your mind requires through meditation.

Meditation is a relaxation technique that can help you cope with stress and the negative impact that stress has on the body. "Meditation can have measurable effects on how the brain functions, even when someone is not actively meditating.

Meditation training has been shown to affect emotional processing in the brain outside of a meditative state, improving emotional stability and response to stress. Meditation also correlates with decreased depression. Findings also suggest that having more compassion towards others may also be beneficial for oneself. Overall, these results are consistent with the hypothesis that meditation may result in enduring, beneficial changes in brain function, especially in the area of emotional processing."
~ Harvard Gazette (Science & Health) -- *Imagining finds different forms of meditation may affect brain structure.*

Always going at a fast pace, stressing over every detail, and continually worrying can keep the body in flight or fight mode. Not good! Meditation on the other hand can help with dopamine and serotonin levels, keeping you calmer and happier.

Meditation Techniques

Sit or lie down with eyes closed and muscles relaxed. Focus on your breathing. Become fully aware of your breathing as you exhale and then inhale.

Think internally, *"I am breathing in and relaxing the top of my head. I am breathing out and keeping the top of my head relaxed.*

I am breathing in and relaxing the back of my head, I am breathing out and keeping the back of my head relaxed.

I am breathing in and relaxing my forehead, I am breathing out and keeping forehead relaxed.

I am breathing in and relaxing my eyes, I am breathing out and keeping eyes relaxed.

I am breathing in and relaxing my face, I am breathing out and keeping my face relaxed.

I am breathing in and relaxing my neck, I am breathing out and keeping my neck relaxed.

I am breathing in and relaxing my shoulders, I am breathing out and keeping my shoulders relaxed all the way down to my toes.

If thoughts crowd your mind or a noise distracts you, inwardly think 'I am releasing all thoughts and expectations' and go back to your breathing.

Then focus on developing positive thoughts and intentions; be aware of how your mind perceives things. Your thoughts will dictate your emotions and mood. If it's raining, do you think 'I can't believe it's raining again, I wish it would just stop' or do you think 'I love it when it rains, it's great for the grass and flowers and sounds beautiful'? Now this might seem unimportant to you. But think about each response and feel how your body reacts to it. The first might make you feel heavy and gloomy, just wanting to go back to bed and pull the blankets over your head. The second might give you a slight smile on your face and make you feel happy to pull out the umbrella and get on with your day.

See how your mood can make a not so nice day seem like a fantastic day full of potential. Your mood then dictates your actions. When you feel happy and positive, you will feel motivated to create a life and situations that will create wonderful possibilities for your day, and for your future. The sky really is limitless.

Keeping your mind consistently on the positive will keep you focused; your body and mind will be relaxed. Then once you've mastered your thoughts, visualize a positive scene. Something you would like to see unfold for you. It can be anything that either makes you happy or could make you happy when it happens. What this will do is bring the things you want or choose for your life to the top of your mind, and you will start doing things that will bring you closer, and eventually to, your desires. If you're thinking you can't, you won't be able to, because you will believe yourself and you won't take the necessary steps to achieving your highest potential of greatness.

I know there will be times when you feel overwhelmed with circumstances that you might not have control over, or that are so painful you can't ever imagine being happy again. I promise you, you can take yourself out of that situation, even if for only a moment. Focus on a pleasant feeling and thought, and away from any thoughts that might bring you pain and/or stress. You have full control over your mind and thoughts. You and no one else.

When things are feeling dark and heavy, that is when you need to focus with all your intention on the positive. Finding a positive thought or situation will take you out of the dark thoughts and feelings that are weighing you down. Even if for a moment, letting yourself focus on the positive will let you feel lighter, both in your mind and in your body.

When Ellen DeGeneres asked 105-year-old Edith, who had just gotten her license renewed that day and was more alert and active than I see most people in their twenties, what her secret was, Edith replied "...I've always been very happy, I feel positive and if something happens that I can't do anything about, I don't let it bother me."

I want to touch once more on the power of forgiveness and leave you with one last thought: Forgiveness and letting go of what you can't change. Feeling anger, hatred, and letting someone or something bring you down only hurts you. You do not have to keep putting yourself in the position to be hurt, or taken advantage of. Simply take yourself out of the situation, away from the person, and then let it go. Negative feelings can cause a knot in your stomach, pinch your shoulders, and even cause backache. So be selfish and forgive others. Forgive, turn the other cheek, and move your thoughts and feelings to more positive people and situations. Make happiness your priority. Ask yourself every day, 'How can I make myself happier?' and just do it. Follow your joy!

Remember the plan is to feel healthy and light, not heavy. This can be accomplished by a change in your food, thoughts, and your perception of events.

DIET AND NUTRITION

When my daughter was young she asked me why I didn't let her eat at fast-food restaurants. I told her that her body and mind were growing on the foods she ate and I wanted them to have the best that they could have. It wasn't until I started to do my research that I would know how right I was.

Our bodies are made up of trillions of cells. They may all have their individual jobs, but in reality our skin, eyes, lungs are all made up of the same thing. Cells. This is when I started to realize the enormous impact that food had on the health of our whole body, not just the target area we are trying to improve. Think about it, when you take any type of pain relief medicine. It's not that the medicine knows to go to the back or the knee or wherever you're feeling the pain. It goes everywhere; you are only focusing on and aware of the area that you feel the pain. Just like medicine, but even better, giving your body the right foods, water and supplements heals the whole body.

Organic Food vs Manufactured Food

"The debate about the advantages of organic foods is over. According to a new $25 million study into organic food -- the largest of its kind to date -- organic food is more nutritious than ordinary produce and it may help to lengthen people's lives and prevent disease."

www.thebestofrawfood.com/advantages-of-organic-foods.html

The cost is the most common deterrent I hear to eating organic food. At first glance, organic food costs approximately one third more than conventionally farmed food. Although organic food might cost more initially, it will save you a whole lot more money in the end. Not to mention you will feel incredible. Once you start to eat organic, you will never want to go back to anything else.

First, it's important to get smart when you shop. When food is cheap, people have a tendency to buy more and waste more. When purchasing organic food, start buying only what you need and making sure you use it. That in itself is going to keep your grocery bill comparable to what you are accustomed to spending. Second, I'm going to show you how to fill your body up with all the nutrients it needs. What this will do is keep you from overeating. If you're not overeating, you'll be buying less and saving more. Not to mention saving your body a lot of extra weight. Third, you're going to become more productive, have less sick days from work, and have more energy. Last, you are going to feel great and be healthier, helping you save on medical bills, aspirin, and various pharmaceutical products.

If you have kids, let them know the benefits of eating healthy and let them know the cost. Make sure to answer all their questions, giving them all the answers they need to make smart choices for themselves. Also, ask them to help you keep them healthy by not wasting. If you talk to them in a way that includes them in the process, they will rise to the occasion.

When my daughter was younger, she came home from grade four and said "Mom, my friend was eating a bag of Cheetos and asked me why I'm skinny." My daughter then hugged me and thanked me for feeding her so well. Children are smart; when you explain things to them logically and rationally, they will get it.

Secondly, if you give your body the nutrients it requires, you won't have those crazy cravings. When you start eating organic food, it has more of what your body needs and less of what your body doesn't need. No matter how much you eat, if it's lacking in nutrients and vitamins that are crucial for your body's optimal health and survival health, your body is going to keep sending out the signal that it's hungry, because you still haven't given it what it requires. You will eat, and eat and eat, not knowing why you have crazy fits of hunger after a large meal.

When you start being kind to your body and giving it the nutrients it requires, you won't be feeling the desire to overeat, because your body is going to be satisfied and happy. Let's start with grass-fed, free range, antibiotic and growth hormone-free meat. In *Maximized Living Nutrition Plans*, by Dr. B.J Hardick, Kimberly Roberto and Dr. Ben Lerner, it states that "Research continues to show that it is not meat that is the problem -- but what we have done to meat. While saturated fat contained in grass-fed meat is critical for brain function, cell function, and the prevention of heart disease, the saturated fat in animals that are fed grains, which is not their preferred source of food, becomes denatured and harmful in the human body. Cows are designed to roam pastures and eat grass, not grain." The same goes for turkey, chickens, eggs, and all other animal products.

I find it ironic that some meat packages are advertising that their animals are corn fed, to fool the consumer with trick advertising to make you think it's a good thing. Corn instead of grass feed changes the animals' metabolic system and makes them unhealthy. A friend of mine who grew up on a farm told me, when her father found a cow in the corn field, he would chase the cow away. Her dad told her it was because corn is like junk food for cows and unhealthy for them. She also said that, when a cow got sick and they had to give it antibiotics, her father would not use the cow or its milk for a year. However, today it's common practice in the non-organic farms to give their cows a steady dose of antibiotics. To top that off, non-organic farms also give their animals growth hormones. Think about it, if the animal is getting growth hormones, so are you. It's getting into your system and can cause a kaleidoscope of problems.

Dairy products in particular should be organic because, if they are not, not only do they have the problems I mentioned above, they also have hidden sugar added to them. Cheese, milk, and butter were some of the first things I changed to organic, and I was shocked at the amazing results from just changing these few things. Try switching and see what happens; the results will be proof in themselves.

Gary LeBanc, author of *Ikkuma Evolution of Vitality,* states that, when he was a Director at a large food corporation, they found a way to take the cheese out of cheese slices. "Cheese was too expensive, so they did a lot of testing to find a way to take it out and make it look and melt the same."

When I started to eat more healthy, I switched to whole wheat instead of white bread. However, I soon realized that sugar is also found in whole wheat as well. A lot of the conventional whole wheat bread out there is whole wheat added to white flour. *Ikkuma Evolution of Vitality* also states that "eating two slices of whole wheat bread is like drinking a can of coke". Whole grain is the way to go. There is much debate on this and some people think that you have to eliminate whole grain altogether. However, I feel that our bodies have evolved enough over time to be able to process whole ancient grains. That being said, too much is not good for you; remember everything in moderation.

> *The European Union-funded study found that organic fruit and vegetables have up to 50% more antioxidants, which scientists believe can cut the risk of cancer and heart disease. They also have more vitamins and minerals, such as iron and zinc.*
> www.helpguide.org/life/organic_foods_pesticides_gmo.htm

"Why do pesticides matter?

In order to use pesticides, conventional farming has to use modified seeds that can withstand the deadly dose of pesticides that would normally kill the fruits and vegetables we eat. This accumulation of pesticides over time builds up in our body and starts to cause malfunctions. Eating organic also helps you avoid putting unwanted chemicals and pesticides in your body.

- Children and fetuses are most vulnerable to pesticide exposure due to their less-developed immune systems and because their bodies and brains are still developing. Exposure at an early age can cause developmental delays, behavioral disorders, and motor dysfunction.
- Pregnant women are more vulnerable due to the added stress pesticides put on their already taxed organs. Plus, pesticides can be passed from mother to child in the womb, as well as through breast milk. Some exposures can cause delayed effects on the nervous system, even years after the initial exposure.
- Most of us have an accumulated build-up of pesticide exposure in our bodies due to numerous years of exposure.

> This chemical "body burden" as it is medically known, could lead to health issues such as headaches, birth defects, and added strain on weakened immune systems."

www.helpingguide.org

The Environmental Protection Agency (EPA) and the U.S. Department of Health & Human Services have determined that, of the 25 most commonly used agricultural pesticides:

- 6 disrupt normal functions of hormones.
- 10 are harmful to reproductive organs.
- 5 are toxic to the nervous system.
- 17 cause genetic damage.
- 18 are harmful to the skin, eyes, and lungs.
- About half are comprised of cancer-causing chemicals.

In 2002, A Consumers Union study found that, of the 12 most commonly eaten produce items and wheat samples, 73% – 90% were contaminated by pesticides, even after washing and peeling.
www.consumersunion.org/food/organicsumm.htm

Tip: When you have an upset stomach, don't reach for that funky pink stuff. Squeeze the juice from a fresh lemon onto a spoon and down the hatch. Lemons are mistakenly thought of as being acidic; however, they actually counter acidity.
http://grandriverorganics.ca

SUGAR

Death by sugar may not be an overstatement—evidence is mounting that sugar is THE MAJOR FACTOR causing obesity and chronic disease. (Dr. Robert H. Lusting, MD)

Because of the difficulty of this step, I want you to take it in two stages. First, let's just start by paying attention to your sugar intake and reducing it.

Fat doesn't make you fat. But sugar that turns into fat will.

Let's work on reducing your sugar intake by avoiding the obvious sugar. A friend of mine was drinking 10 - 12 cans of pop a day. He started by reducing his pop intake to two cans a day, which is a fantastic start. Lets start to think about it. He was actully able to reduced his sugar intake by around 100 to 130 spoons of sugar each day. In the first two months of following my health tips, he lost 23 pounds. You may not have one obvious item, it might be a few. That's okay; eliminate as many of them as possible.

My sweet temptations were chocolate bars. Whenever I was at the gas station and saw that chocolate bars were on sale, which seemed to be all the time, I'd grab a bunch. After all, it was two or three for a dollar. It was hard for the first three weeks that I went without them. Yet, I survived and I no longer crave or want any of my old so-called treats.

Stop the bad habits now! Step by step, you will start looking and feeling great. If you drink coffee with sugar, stop and think of how many spoons of sugar that adds up to in a day. Then start to drink your coffee black. I use high fat organic milk or cream. Stevia in its natural form is a great substitute for sugar. My favourite is honey; in its raw form it tastes divine in coffee and is a great way to sweeten your smoothies in the morning. I occasionally consume cane sugar or organic sugar when it's found in organic foods. Although it should be used in moderation.

You also need to stop saying "a little won't hurt". Because, if you start paying attention every time you say it, you will soon realize a little here and a little there adds up fast!

When you want to snack on something, have a glass of water. If you're still hungry, grab an apple, or what I like to do is have a bowl of pumpkin seeds, walnuts, or some other healthy alternative on my counter and ready to go. Also getting some fresh vegetables and preparing them ahead of time really helps. What you need to do is go shopping and grab the vegetables you like. As soon as you get home, wash, cut, and put them in little snack-sized containers. Then, instead of reaching for chips or cookies, you can reach for them. It's a healthier and tastier alternative. It's all about being prepared.

In 1957, Dr. William Coda Martin classified refined sugar as a poison. Today the average North American is ingesting over 50 spoons of sugar a day.

We've talked about paying attention to your sugar intake. Now comes the hard part. It's time to eliminate processed sugar from your diet altogether.

I read that the same method is used in making processed sugar as it was in making heroin.

Think about it; why is it that you crave, have to have, go out of your way to stop those sugar cravings? You're giving yourself your fix. You're a sugar addict.

Sugar is detrimental to your health. It is a foreign substance that your body has no idea what to do with. When I think of sugar, I picture watered down rat poison, to help keep me from getting tempted. It may not kill you instantly. It's worse; it's a slow, prolonged, and painful death.

Dr. David Reuben, author of *Everything You Always Wanted to Know About Nutrition*, says white refined sugar is not a food. It is a pure chemical extracted from plant sources, purer in fact than cocaine, which it resembles in many ways. Its true name is sucrose and its chemical formula is C12H22O11.

> *Sugar promotes cancer. Feeding cancer cells their primary fuel is like pouring gas on a fire.*
>
> *Maximized Living Nutrition Plans*
> by Dr. Hardick, Kimberly Roberto, and Dr. Lerner

Good sugar vs. bad sugar and how to look for hidden processed sugar: this is difficult, as sugar is hidden in many foods we wouldn't even imagine. Here is my simple tip to keep you from becoming overwhelmed. Start reading the labels, not for low-fat, low-calorie marketing tricks. The only thing I read a label for is ingredients. If I see sugar as an ingredient, no matter the amount, I put it down and don't even think twice. You will be shocked by how many of your so-called healthy foods have this one killer substance.

Once you have eliminated it from your diet, you will realize how good you feel. The exception to the rule is, 'organic sugar', 'cane sugar', 'honey' or 'stevia'. These are all natural sugars that the body can digest and are a sweet and tasty alternative to help keep you healthy, without completely giving up sweet treats.

It gets easier as you go. Remember it is a step by step process. But it will become especially easy as you notice the dramatic changes in your body. Not just how great you look in your jeans or that outfit you couldn't wear for years, but how much better you feel inside and out.

As you eliminate processed sugar from your diet, you're going to wonder how you ever lived feeling the way you did. That feeling of bloating, gut rot, uneasiness in your body is NOT normal and you're going to feel so alive, so light and so free. Not to mention that awful feeling of constipation will be a thing of the past.

At this point, your body will go through a natural detox. You may get a little rash or you may start to see a black tar-like substance ooze out of your pores. This is all natural, as your body is now going to be flushing out all that bad toxic waste that it's been holding onto. As you start your natural detoxing, you're going to be adding years, and a more youthful feeling, to your life!

Sugar trends for the past 300 years

Not only has the sugar we've been ingesting changed in the past 300 years, so has the amount we consume.

"In 1700, the average person consumed about four pounds of sugar per year. In 1800, the average person consumed about 18 pounds of sugar per year. In 1900, the average person consumed about 90 pounds of sugar per year. In 2009, the average person consumed about 180 pounds of sugar per year."

www.wholevegan.com/refined_sugar_history.html

We wonder why obesity has become rampant throughout the world. The great news about obesity, and the illnesses that come from it, is that they are man-made and very preventable.

Summary

- Sugar promotes premature aging.
- Sugar can cause hormonal and metabolic imbalance.
- Sugar promotes diabetes.
- Sugar increases the acidity of the body. (All disease thrives in acidic environments.)
- Sugar can cause inflammation.
- Sugar is the primary reason for high cholesterol.
- Sugar leads to heart disease.
- Sugar is a toxin.
- Cancer feeds off sugar.

When cigarettes first came out, clever marketing labeled them healthy. However, we now know the consequences of smoking and some countries even make manufacturers label the packages to warn of the deadly effects smoking has on the human body.

Today there are certain foods and supplements that clever marketing advertisers have labeled as healthy, or ironically labeled as food.

We've all been tricked to eat a low-fat, low-cholesterol diet. Yet the human population is getting larger. Clothing manufacturers have actually changed the labeling sizes on clothing to make us think we are smaller than we are, and obesity has now been labeled a disease by the American Medical Association.

WATER

You have the fountain of youth right at your kitchen tap, and it's free!

Make sure you don't pass this chapter thinking that you drink enough water or that you think you know all the benefits it has. Although it is simple, it can have a profound affect on your health.

Did you know that water gives you more energy than caffeinated drinks?!

Our bodies consist of 75 - 80% water. Yet are you drinking enough of it? Probably not. Most people are dehydrated. Think about it; your skin, your hair, your organs, and your neurological system all need water to function. However, our bodies are built for survival. What happens when you're not getting enough water is that your body is going to send it to only to the parts of the body that need it to survive, and deprive the rest.

There is no magic number I can tell you on how much to drink, as all our bodies are different and everyone is experiencing a different level of dehydration. Your job is to see how much water it takes for you to make your urine clear. It's that simple. If your urine is yellow or has odour to it, it means you're dehydrated.

I know it's going to seem impossible to drink enough water, but it's not. I find, as long as I keep a large glass of water by my side all day, I'm going to drink it. Even if you don't like water, which at one point I didn't. Make yourself drink it anyway. I guarantee you will grow to like it and even crave it. Drink what you can and slowly add more each day.

My friends who started drinking more water came back to me and stated "I can't believe what a difference drinking more water did. I'm smiling, have more energy, less headaches, and feel so much better already."

Now if that isn't enough for you, let me explain it this way. Your body needs water. If it's not getting it on a regular basis, your body is going to store it, creating a bloating feeling and adding to your body mass because it's saying 'I'd better save this because I don't know when I'm going to get any more!' Water is an important part of your body's functioning. For one, your body needs water to absorb nutrients and flush out unwanted toxins. You wouldn't allow your car to go without oil, so why would you deprive your body of water?

Water serves as a lubricant for our joints, and lessons the burden on our kidneys and liver by flushing out waste products. It regulates the body temperature and helps prevent constipation. Furthermore, water helps the body absorb nutrients and helps send them and oxygen to our cells. It also protects our organs and tissues. Even our lungs need water, and a lack of water can be the cause of some asthma.

Our muscles consist of 75% water, and our brain consists of 90% water. Bone is 22% water and blood 83%. It's time to start giving your body what it needs to survive at its prime.

Okay, I think by now most of you got the point. But for those of you who are still fighting me, here are some more reasons to keep drinking water all day long.

There are numerous studies that show drinking water can help reduce the risk of cancer, heart attacks, and migraines.

Drinking water also helps with weight loss, clears your skin and gives it a healthier glow.

So ... you're going to carry a glass or bottle of water with you all day long. However, I will warn you. A friend who followed my drinking water advice was in a two-hour conference call, wiggling and squirming the whole time. Make sure to time it right and take regular bathroom breaks. I also learned the hard way; if you don't want to wake up and have to run to the bathroom all night long, stop drinking water a couple hours before bed.

As you're starting your water challenge, your body is going to start flushing out all that extra water it's been storing. For the first three weeks, you will be flushing it all out every half hour or so. This is normal and, as your body becomes hydrated and at its ultimate level, this will slow down. You'll also find any unwanted bloating in the face or body will start to disappear.

Remember water is free, it is easily accessible, and it keeps your body working at a higher level. So drink up, because you deserve to look and feel great!

Tip: Place a cooler of water in your office, and have water jars ready to go in the fridge. I keep a large glass jar of water (this could also be a mason jar) with a lid, full at all times by my side. Add lemon wedges, mint leaves or cucumber for a change. Never add powder or liquid flavouring, as this will eliminate all the beneficial results you're trying to accomplish.

Summary of Water

- Your brain consists of 90% water.
- Water serves as a lubricant for your joints.
- Water lessens the burden on your kidneys and liver by flushing out waste products.
- Water regulates the body temperature.
- Water helps prevent constipation.
- Water helps the body absorb nutrients and helps send them and oxygen to your cells.
- Water protects your organs and tissues.
- Your muscles consist of 75% water.
- Your bones consists of 22% water.

SUPPLEMENTS

Regardless of whether or not you are suffering from a head injury, cod liver oil is a great supplement to take on a daily basis. Dr. Ben Kim, Natural Health Solutions, Inc (drbenkim.com) states that "cod liver oil is one of the most reliable and concentrated food sources of four nutrients that are essential to our health: DHA, EPA, vitamin A, and vitamin D. These four nutrients are needed for:

- Healthy skin
- Strong bones and teeth
- Healthy joints
- A healthy cardiovascular system
- A healthy nervous system and prevention of depression and other mood disorders, as well as a healthy digestive tract

After waking up two weeks after I started taking the supplements prescribed by the naturopathic doctor and realizing the benefits they had on my health, I started to question what other foods I could add to keep improving my recovery, and what foods I could remove from my diet that might be hindering the healing process.

Did you know that there are over 3,000 deaths a year from prescription drugs? I bet you would be hard-pressed to find a death due to a healthy lifestyle. I know that last sentence sounds a little silly. But, not as silly as not giving your body what it needs to be the healthiest and best version of itself it can be.

One of the major vitamins your body needs is Vitamin C. Your body can't make it or store it; therefore, it is important to add Vitamin C to your diet on a daily basis. I use one large orange or two medium size oranges to make fresh orange juice every morning. It's a refreshing way to start the day.

Try to avoid supplemental vitamins from the pharmacy, when you can get them from a natural source. However, if you do use supplemental vitamins, make sure they're from a health food store and read the labels. You don't want to inadvertently ingest unhealthy substances that are added to the supplements.

Ikkuma has come out with a new supplement called 'Limitless'. Limitless is a safe, natural dietary supplement.

(www.ikkuma.com)

Vitamin D helps build strong bones, boosts immune systems, and much more. We all know the important role Vitamin D plays; however, the biggest challenge is how to obtain it. I remember a time when skin cancer became a scare. The 'Theys' ('They' - are a source of unknown origin; however, using 'they say' in a sentence seems to create a false sense of truth. e.g. They say that fat is bad for you.) were hard at work informing us about the danger of exposing our skin to the sun and, presto, once it was out in the public as a matter of fact, sunscreen and tanning beds popped up everywhere. Tanning beds were considered 'The Safe Sun' and sunscreen was thought of as a daily must. That's why I was blown away in university when I learned that, ten years after we as a society had become aware of the sun and its so-called damaging rays, skin cancer was no longer just a threat in old age; skin cancer had become more prominent in the young. I can't tell you what to do but, when I started to connect the dots, I started to think for myself. I get at least 15-20 mintes of sun a day. If it's overcast and the sun is not exposed, I take an all-natural Vitamin D supplement. I also make sure not to overexpose my skin to the sun, preventing sunburns. However, the most important thing I do is what I don't do. I do not use tanning beds, sunscreens or other body sprays.

Now let's talk about the low-fat diet myth that we have been brainwashed with by the 'Theys'. Think of it this way: we are surrounded in North America with low-fat/low-calorie diets, yet the obesity rate is so high that it is now labeled a disease. Something is off. WE NEED FAT! The fat in grass-fed organic beef is good for you. The fat in organic sour cream and in unpasteurized organic whole milk is good for you, as are many other good fats.

I often wonder if our low-fat diets are putting our brains in greater risk of head injury than if we had a well-balanced good-fat filled diet. Dr. Amen from the Amen Clinics states "DHA, one form of omega-3 fatty acids found in fish, makes up a large portion of the grey matter of the brain."

> *In France, the levels of saturated fat intake are much higher than they are in the United States, yet the French and Spanish have much lower rates of death from cardiovascular disease.*
>
> *Maximized Living Nutrition Plans*
> by Dr. Hardick, Kimberly Roberto, and Dr. Lerner

MAGNESIUM: EARTH'S MIRACLE HEALER

"Your body is your temple." Your body houses your soul, and how you treat your body determines how long, how healthy, and how happy you are from day to day. We come from the earth, we are of the earth and the earth provides us with everything we need to be well. One of the many blessings of this earth is magnesium. Magnesium is this wonderful magical substance that truly will work miracles on your body, and it comes from the sea.

Magnesium is the fourth most abundant mineral found in human cells and stabilizes cell membranes. A deficiency in magnesium is devastating to the wellbeing of the human body.

Arthritis, back pain, headache and insomnia are only a few of the things I've seen magnesium aid in. 'Then why haven't you heard about it' or only minimally? That's the same question I've been asking myself since I've found this wonder substance that mother nature has provided for us. The only answer I have for you is money. It's cheap and hard to make a buck off of. However there are some wonderful companies where you can find it, such as Natural Calm Canada, whose profits go to support orphans and their communities through Organics 4 Orphans. Go to www.organics4orphans.org to read up on some of the wonderful work they do!

Magnesium is the number one substance I share with everyone. Without fail it continues to help others in so many amazing ways.

The benefits are truly out of this world. The cost is so minimal that there is no reason you shouldn't be using it! It's just a matter of incorporating it into your lifestyle and remembering to take a little every day.

This tip is going to make you feel great, and get rid of many of your aches and pains. Not only did it help in the recovery of my Post Concussion Symptoms, but it also helped many other unpleasant discomforts I had been experiencing.

For years I had chronic calf cramps and, no matter what I did, they wouldn't go away. However, after reading *Transdermal Magnesium Therapy* by Dr. Mark Sircus, I started to rub a little magnesium oil into my calfs. The cramps went away instantly. I also had stiff, sore fingers. I thought it was just from writing all the time. However, by rubbing the magnesium into my legs, I got it on my fingers as well. Presto, my fingers were better too. I didn't even realize, before I started with the magnesium, how bad my fingers were, until the stiffness went away.

At first I had to use the magnesium oil every half hour or so. Then every few hours, then once a day. Now as long as I rub a little magnesium oil into my fingers and calfs once or twice a week, I'm fine. This, combined with a daily dose of magnesium drops, works for me. However, I will get into the different methods of adding magnesium to your daily routine in a moment. First I want to explain to you why it's so important.

Magnesium deficiency can affect virtually every system of the body.

> *Without sufficient magnesium, the body accumulates toxins and acid residues, and thusly degenerates more rapidly and ages prematurely.*
> *Transdermal Magnesium Therapy* by Mark Sircus, Ac., O.M.D.

Our body needs magnesium, like it needs water.

> *Every organ, bone and cell needs magnesium. Your heart, muscles, and kidneys especially. As well, magnesium is important in the function of enzymes, energy production, and helps your body absorb calcium, copper, zinc, potassium, vitamin D, and other essential nutrients.*
> University of Maryland Medical Center

Magnesium is the energy our cells use to reproduce themselves, and remember, every part of our body is made up of cells. Magnesium helps the body heal itself by giving our healthy cells the needed energy to reproduce themselves, and is crucial to a healthy immune system. My dad, seventy five at the time, started to put a little magnesium oil onto his hands every day at my request. Something incredible and unforeseen happened once he started to do this. Since he was a teenager, he had painful eczema on his hands. No medication or lotion prescribed by his doctor worked. He wore bandages on his fingers every day. The magnesium completely cured his eczema. When my dad forgets to put magnesium on for an extended time, the eczema comes back. It is important to keep the magnesium up on a daily basis.

Low levels of magnesium can also effect mood, temper, and can contribute to depression and anxiety. One friend I've been helping suffers from depression, mood swings, and a personality disorder. She has found that taking her daily intake of magnesium has helped her mind feel clearer, and keeps her clam. When she forgets to take it, she says she feels confused and cloudy again.

I've also helped two other friends who suffer from insomnia. One is a forty-five year-old man, the other a high school student. All they had to do was drink a warm magnesium drink at night and they slept soundly.

Magnesium is a mineral found in your body. About 50% of it is found in your bones, and the other half is found mostly inside your body's tissue and organ cells, with 1% in your blood.

Again, our body needs magnesium like it needs water. Only in different amounts, and for different purposes.

Magnesium deficiency can affect almost every system in your body. One of the many things magnesium does is it helps your body absorb the nutrients it needs. For example, without magnesium, your body can't properly absorb calcium. Take my chronic leg cramps. I had nurses and doctors who kept saying that I must be low in calcium. So I did whatever I could to add calcium to my diet.

Our body needs the equivalent amount of magnesium to calcium, in order to absorb the calcium into our system. Before I go into the different types of magnesium out there, I want to make sure you know how important magnesium is in your body's functioning and why it needs it. The more information you have on why it's so important, the more likely you will be to keep adding it to your daily routine.

Magnesium helps maintain normal muscle and nerve function, keeps your heart rhythm steady, and keeps your bones strong. Unfortunately, our foods today have 75% less magnesium than they once did, due to our fields being overcropped and stripped of their nutrients. It's important to supplement your intake on a daily basis. At one point, I was feeling so great that I thought I didn't need to take my daily dose of magnesium anymore. My symptoms all ended up coming back. Magnesium seems to play an important role in a healthier, happier, and longer life.

"Magnesium is needed for more than 300 biochemical reactions in the body. It helps maintain normal muscle and nerve function, keeps heart rhythm steady, supports a healthy immune system, and keeps bones strong. Magnesium also helps regulate blood sugar levels, promotes normal blood pressure, and is known to be involved in energy metabolism and protein synthesis. There is an increased interest in the role of magnesium in preventing and managing disorders such as hypertension, cardiovascular disease, and diabetes. Dietary magnesium is absorbed in the small intestines, and is excreted through kidneys."

Office of Dietary Supplements - National Institutes of Health

White blood cells and other immune components are sensitive to malnutrition, especially when it comes to magnesium.

Transdermal Magnesium Therapy by Mark Sircus, Ac., O.M.D.

The first product I took to increase my magnesium levels was magnesium drops. Most people are deficient in magnesium, and the drops are a good way to start. What I do is put the recommended amount of drops in a shot glass with a little bit of water or orange juice to mask the taste. The bottle indicates a glass of water, but I find a shot glass gets it over and done with faster. It's also important to have something ready to wash it down with. I do this in the morning and then again at night. Our bodies can only absorb so much at one time. A little on the temples helps as well.

Then there is the powder form, which tastes much better than the drops. I like drinking this in hot water at night. Do not take it during the day, as the powder helps for a good night's sleep and you don't want to fall asleep behind the wheel of your car. Although if you put only a quarter of the recommended amount into a bottle of water you can sip it through the day and it will provide you with more energy. Just make sure not to put too much in.

For seniors or people with digestive problems, the magnesium drops and the powder are not a good choice. It's harder for your body to absorb nutrients internally. The best way for you is magnesium oil or gel, as you can absorb it through your skin. It is also the safest way to get magnesium into your system without taking too much, as your skin will stop absorbing it once it has the required amount. However this should not be an issue as most people's magnesium levels are too low to even worry about it.

You can put a couple ounces of magnesium oil into your bath, which relaxes your muscles. Putting magnesium oil on your skin directly will cause irritation. This irritation is not bad for you, just uncomfortable. What I like to do is put it in a spray bottle and dilute it with half water. If you find that putting half water and half magnesium oil still irritates your skin, add a bit more water until you find a comfortable blend.

You can spray the oil or rub the gel into any sore or stiff muscles and joints. It will help relieve the pain and stiffness. This is what eliminated my leg and finger cramps. When I have a headache, I spray a bit over my shoulders and rub it in, as it relaxes the muscles.

This is also what I recommend for kids. You can put it into their baths or spray a little on the back of their hand on a daily basis. It's just as important for them as it is for you. There is also the powder form for kids, which, like for you, can be given to them as a warm drink before bed. It's a nice relaxing drink for them to have while you're reading them a bedtime story.

MIGHTY MAGNESIUM: This overlooked nutrient fights against heart disease, pain and diabetes. US Weekend Magazine Issue Date: September 1, 2002 - Eat Smart - Jean Carper

Readers constantly ask me, "Am I getting enough calcium?" They rarely ask, "Am I getting enough magnesium?" Yet that may be the most critical nutritional question of the moment. Americans' intake of magnesium dropped 50% in the last century, and the consequences are alarming. A lack of magnesium underlies our epidemic of heart disease, high blood pressure, diabetes and osteoporosis, says Larence Resnick, M.D., a professor of medicine at Cornell Medical Center. Minus magnesium, hearts beat irregularly; arteries stiffen, constrict and clog; blood pressure rises; blood tends to clot; muscles spasm; insulin grows weaker and blood sugar jumps; bones lose strength; and pain signals intensify.

"Many people needlessly suffer pain -- including fibromyalgia, migraines and muscle cramps -- because they don't get enough magnesium," says Mildred Seeling, M.D., magnesium researcher, University of North Carolina.

Many people worsen the problem by loading up on calcium, which flushes magnesium out of cells, Resnick says. He urges getting at least 1 milligram of magnesium for each 2mg of calcium.

10 important ways it helps

1. **Heart arrhythmias.** "People need to know magnesium deficiency predisposes them to serious, even deadly, heart arrhythmias" -- irregular and abnormally fast heartbeats or atrial fibrillation -- says cardiac specialist Michael Brodsky at the Collage of Medicine of the University of California, Irvine. In a British study, taking magnesium daily for six weeks reduced arrhythmias between 25% and 50%. In new U.S. Deparment of Agriculture tests, women skimping on magnesium developed irregular heartbeats within three months. Supplements corrected the abnormality.

2. **Blocked arteries.** High blood magnesium cuts your odds of dying from common "ischemic" heart disease (blocked or narrowed arteries) by one-third, say researchers at the Centers for Disease Control and Prevention. In other research, magnesium shortages lower good HDL cholesterol and accelerate hardening of the arteries.

3. **Blood pressure.** Cornell's Lawrence Resnick recently documented that, the higher the magnesium inside your cells, the more apt you are to have lower blood pressure, more elastic blood vessels and a less enlarged heart. He calls magnesium a natural calcium-channel blocker (blood-pressure drug) and says supplements can help normalize blood pressure.

4. **Diabetes.** "Diabetes is a magnesium deficiency state," says Jerry Nadler, M.D., University Virginia School of Medicine. He finds 80% of diabetics have low intracellular magnesium. Indeed, research suggests low magnesium boosts your risk of developing type 2 diabetes by one-third. He says supplements can improve insulin activity and may cut diabetes' risk and complications. Some specialists tell diabetics to take 400mg magnesium daily.

5. **Strong bones.** Magnesium is as vital as calcium in preventing osteoporosis, says the University of North Carolina's Mildred Seelig: It's essential for normal bone metabolism. In a Swedish study, magnesium, but not calcium, helped prevent hip fractures in older women. Tufts researchers found high magnesium intake predicted higher bone mass and less bone loss in older people.

6. **Migraines.** Half of migraine sufferers have low magnesium, and upping magnesium has reduced the duration and intensity, and frequency dropped 42% in German adults who took 600mg magnesium daily for a month. Italian children given 122mg to 366mg magnesium daily had two-thirds fewer migraines after a month.

7. **Sound sleep.** Several studies show a lack of magnesium can alter electrical activity in the brain, causing agitated sleep and frequent awakenings. "It looks like magnesium is important for a good night's sleep," says USDA researcher Forrest H. Nielsen.

8. **Safer pregnancy.** Extensive research shows that magnesium lessens pre-eclampsia, in which blood pressure soars in late pregnancy, upping the risk of spontaneous abortions and premature, low birth-weight babies. A large new British study of 10,000 women in 33 countries confirms that taking magnesium sulphate supplements reduced the hazard by 50%.

9. **Pain relief.** If you have leg cramps or other muscle cramps, taking 100mg to 400mg magnesium daily may bring relief, Seelig says. Extra magnesium also may help prevent or relieve painful myalgias (including the syndrome known as fibromyalgia), chronic lower back pain, restless legs syndrome, erythromelalgia (a painful dilation of skin blood vessels) and chronic fatigue syndrome. Seelig says magnesium reduces a pain transmitter in the nervous system called substance P.

10. **Extra benefits.** Taking magnesium could counteract the heart attack and stroke hazards of hormone replacement therapy. Seelig says: "research shows magnesium counters estrogen's clot-producing abilities." Further, magnesium may help treat premature ejaculation and relieve symptoms of premenstrual syndrome.

How much do you need?

The recommended daily allowance for magnesium is 320mg for women, 400mg for men. Many authorities take a 400mg magnesium supplement daily. Possible side effects: diarrhea or loose stools. "It's no big deal," Seelig says, because the body usually adapts, or you can cut back. Avoid magnesium supplements if you have kidney disease. Alcohol, diuretics or high doses of calcium all deplete magnesium.

Now that you are fully aware of how great it feels to eat healthily and think positively, you will be able to listen to your body tell you what it wants in order to be the healthiest version of you that you can be.

Once you've been doing this for a good few months, don't forget to go back and read your answers to the health questionnaire you did at the beginning of this book section. You will be amazed at how far you have come and how great you feel.

Part Three
Your Health

HEALTH QUESTIONNAIRE

Answer these questions before you get started on your own road to optimum health. It's for your private records; make sure to be honest. Once you're at your peak health, looking back at your questionnaire will help reinforce what you've learned. It will remind you of how far you have come and how important maintaining your healthy lifestyle is.

1. How do you feel physically on a regular basis?

2. How do you feel mentally the majority of the time?

3. How often do you get sick? Explain.

4. Is your mind clear or foggy most of the time?

5. How do you feel emotionally most of the time?

6. How would you like to feel?

7. What do you want to accomplish with your new healthy lifestyle?

8. Check off all that pertain to you and explain how they affect your daily life:

    - Headaches / Migraines
    - Back pain. Where is it located?
    - High / Low blood pressure
    - Cramps? Legs, fingers, stomach etc.

9. Have you ever suffered from cancer? Or other life- threatening diseases?

10. Do you eat a high-processed food / junk diet? How many times a day or week?

11. Are you on the road frequently?

12. How often do you eat vegetables?
 ___________ a week.

13. How often do you eat seeds or nuts?
 ___________ a week.

14. How often do you eat fresh fruit?
 ___________ a week.

15. Do you have more than 3 servings of caffeine daily?
 Yes____ No____

16. Do you have more than 7 alcoholic drinks weekly?
 Yes____ No____

17. How much do you work out per day?
 none ____
 10-20 min ____
 20-30 min ____
 30-40 min____
 Other (explain) ______________________________________

18. Check off all of the following that pertain to you:
 - ○ chronic intestinal disease, ulcers, Crohn's, irritable bowel
 - ○ frquent diarrhea or constipation
 - ○ asthma or wheezing
 - ○ PMS or menstrual cramps
 - ○ eczema
 - ○ anxiety
 - ○ indifference or apathy, lack of interest
 - ○ chronic fatigue
 - ○ dry mouth

- very fast heart beats, irregular heart beats, or arrhythmia
- overactive thyroid, or parathyroid gland
- diabetes
- numbness in face, hands, or feet
- frequently too hot or too cold
- face pale, puffy, or lacking in colour
- bloating

19. Anything else you feel is relevant?

HEALING MIND AND BODY JOURNAL

This journal will help you keep track of your progress. It will also help keep you motivated and moving forward.

You will notice that I don't touch on physical fitness and exercise in my book, and there is a reason for that. The book is about teaching you what I have learned to get to where I am today. Unfortunately for me, due to my accident, I am starting at Ground Zero when it comes to fitness. This is not by choice and I wish with all my heart that I could still be running 45 minutes a day and taking various classes.

However the great news is that it has reminded me of what it was like to start from Ground Zero and what it takes to move to the next level.

First, let's go into what it does not take. It does not take pushing yourself so hard that you vomit, can't move the next day, or feel the burn so much that you can't get through your work day.

Of course, you want to try to achieve a little more every day, but if you push yourself too hard it's not good for you. You want to enjoy working out, have fun with it and look forward to it. That is what is going to make it a lifestyle for you and not just a spontaneous once and in a while thing.

AND finally, change it up! Go from kayaking, to boot camps to boxing lessons. When you were a kid, was there some activity you really wanted to do, but your parents (for whatever reason) didn't put you in? So do it now, take karate lessons, dance lessons, ski lessons, and just go for it. Get fit and have fun all at the same time. It could be as simple as getting a yoga DVD, even if you can only do two or three minutes of it at the begining, that's okay. It's a start; and just try to add a little more every day. Think of how great you're going to feel when that the day comes, and it will, when you can finish the whole DVD or program.

Preplan your meals and your fitness. Keeping organized will help keep you moving forward.

MONTH: __________

DAY ONE:

Often it's the deepest pain which empowers you to grow into your highest self ~ Unknown

Daily Meditation and Gratitude List:

Daily Fitness:

Nutritious Snacks:

Breakfast:

Lunch:

Dinner:

How do you feel today? Mind and Body:

DAY TWO:

Peace is the result of retraining your mind to process life as it is, rather than as you think it should be ~ Wayne W. Dyer

Daily Meditation and Gratitude List:

Daily Fitness:

Nutritious Snacks:

Breakfast:

Lunch:

Dinner:

How do you feel today? Mind and Body:

DAY THREE:

Challenges are what make life interesting and overcoming them is what makes life meaningful ~ Joshua J. Marine

Daily Meditation and Gratitude List:

Daily Fitness:

Nutritious Snacks:

Breakfast:

Lunch:

Dinner:

How do you feel today? Mind and Body:

DAY FOUR:

The words you speak become the house you live in ~ Hafiz

Daily Meditation and Gratitude List:

Daily Fitness:

Nutritious Snacks:

Breakfast:

Lunch:

Dinner:

How do you feel today? Mind and Body:

DAY FIVE:

You are braver than you believe, stronger than you seem, and smarter than you think ~ Winnie the Pooh

Daily Meditation and Gratitude List:

Daily Fitness:

Nutritious Snacks:

Breakfast:

Lunch:

Dinner:

How do you feel today? Mind and Body:

DAY SIX:

There are only two ways to live your life. One is as though nothing is a miracle. The other is as though everything is a miracle

~ Albert Einstein

Daily Meditation and Gratitude List:

Daily Fitness:

Nutritious Snacks:

Breakfast:

Lunch:

Dinner:

How do you feel today? Mind and Body:

DAY SEVEN:

Allow nature to teach you stillness ~ Eckhart Tolle

Daily Meditation and Gratitude List:

Daily Fitness:

Nutritious Snacks:

Breakfast:

Lunch:

Dinner:

How do you feel today? Mind and Body:

DAY EIGHT:

Imperfection is Beauty, Madness is Genius, And it's better to be Absolutely Ridiculous than Absolutely Boring ~ Unknown

Daily Meditation and Gratitude List:

Daily Fitness:

Nutritious Snacks:

Breakfast:

Lunch:

Dinner:

How do you feel today? Mind and Body:

DAY NINE:

Learn how to be happy with what you have while you pursue all that you want ~ Jim Rohn

Daily Meditation and Gratitude List:

Daily Fitness:

Nutritious Snacks:

Breakfast:

Lunch:

Dinner:

How do you feel today? Mind and Body:

DAY TEN:

Kind Words can be short and easy to speak, but their echoes are truly endless ~ Mother Teresa

Daily Meditation and Gratitude List:

Daily Fitness:

Nutritious Snacks:

Breakfast:

Lunch:

Dinner:

How do you feel today? Mind and Body:

DAY ELEVEN:

Be so good they can't ignore you ~ Steve Martin

Daily Meditation and Gratitude List:

Daily Fitness:

Nutritious Snacks:

Breakfast:

Lunch:

Dinner:

How do you feel today? Mind and Body:

DAY TWELVE:

Think, Do, Be, Positive! ~ Unknown

Daily Meditation and Gratitude List:

Daily Fitness:

Nutritious Snacks:

Breakfast:

Lunch:

Dinner:

How do you feel today? Mind and Body:

DAY THIRTEEN:

Inner Peace comes when you no longer rely on the external environment to create your happiness for you.
~ Spirit Science and Metaphysics

Daily Meditation and Gratitude List:

Daily Fitness:

Nutritious Snacks:

Breakfast:

Lunch:

Dinner:

How do you feel today? Mind and Body:

DAY FOURTEEN:

Think about your blessings more than you talk about your problems ~
Spirit Science and Metaphysics

Daily Meditation and Gratitude List:

Daily Fitness:

Nutritious Snacks:

Breakfast:

Lunch:

Dinner:

How do you feel today? Mind and Body:

DAY FIFTEEN:

Embrace the joy and happiness in your life, let the rest fall away.

Daily Meditation and Gratitude List:

Daily Fitness:

Nutritious Snacks:

Breakfast:

Lunch:

Dinner:

How do you feel today? Mind and Body:

DAY SIXTEEN:

Where there is love there is life ~ Mahatma Gandhi

Daily Meditation and Gratitude List:

Daily Fitness:

Nutritious Snacks:

Breakfast:

Lunch:

Dinner:

How do you feel today? Mind and Body:

DAY SEVENTEEN:

In order to carry a positive action we must develop here a positive vision. ~ Dalai Lama

Daily Meditation and Gratitude List:

Daily Fitness:

Nutritious Snacks:

Breakfast:

Lunch:

Dinner:

How do you feel today? Mind and Body:

DAY EIGHTEEN:

The greatest prayer is patience ~ Buddha

Daily Meditation and Gratitude List:

Daily Fitness:

Nutritious Snacks:

Breakfast:

Lunch:

Dinner:

How do you feel today? Mind and Body:

DAY NINETEEN:

Be in Love with your life. Every minute of it ~ Unknown

Daily Meditation and Gratitude List:

Daily Fitness:

Nutritious Snacks:

Breakfast:

Lunch:

Dinner:

How do you feel today? Mind and Body:

DAY TWENTY:

Say YES and you'll figure it out Afterwards ~ Tina Fey

Daily Meditation and Gratitude List:

Daily Fitness:

Nutritious Snacks:

Breakfast:

Lunch:

Dinner:

How do you feel today? Mind and Body:

DAY TWENTY-ONE:

The Secret to health for both mind and body is not to mourn for the past, Worry about the future, or anticipate troubles, but to live in the present moment wisely and earnestly ~ Buddha

Daily Meditation and Gratitude List:

Daily Fitness:

Nutritious Snacks:

Breakfast:

Lunch:

Dinner:

How do you feel today? Mind and Body:

DAY TWENTY-TWO:

A Good Laugh and a Long Sleep are the two best cures for anything ~
Irish Proverb

Daily Meditation and Gratitude List:

Daily Fitness:

Nutritious Snacks:

Breakfast:

Lunch:

Dinner:

How do you feel today? Mind and Body:

DAY TWENTY-THREE:

There is always something to be thankful for.

Daily Meditation and Gratitude List:

Daily Fitness:

Nutritious Snacks:

Breakfast:

Lunch:

Dinner:

How do you feel today? Mind and Body:

DAY TWENTY-FOUR:

Every accomplishment begins with a decision to try ~ Unknown

Daily Meditation and Gratitude List:

Daily Fitness:

Nutritious Snacks:

Breakfast:

Lunch:

Dinner:

How do you feel today? Mind and Body:

DAY TWENTY-FIVE:

If you want to know where your heart is, look to where your mind goes when it wanders ~ Unknown

Daily Meditation and Gratitude List:

Daily Fitness:

Nutritious Snacks:

Breakfast:

Lunch:

Dinner:

How do you feel today? Mind and Body:

DAY TWENTY-SIX:
Everyone Smiles in the same Language.

Daily Meditation and Gratitude List:

Daily Fitness:

Nutritious Snacks:

Breakfast:

Lunch:

Dinner:

How do you feel today? Mind and Body:

DAY TWENTY-SEVEN:

When you realize how perfect everything is you will tilt your head back and laugh at the sky ~ Buddha

Daily Meditation and Gratitude List:

Daily Fitness:

Nutritious Snacks:

Breakfast:

Lunch:

Dinner:

How do you feel today? Mind and Body:

DAY TWENTY-EIGHT:

A jug fills drop by drop ~ Buddha

Daily Meditation and Gratitude List:

Daily Fitness:

Nutritious Snacks:

Breakfast:

Lunch:

Dinner:

How do you feel today? Mind and Body:

DAY TWENTY-NINE:

What Matters Most is How You See Yourself ~ Unknown

Daily Meditation and Gratitude List:

Daily Fitness:

Nutritious Snacks:

Breakfast:

Lunch:

Dinner:

How do you feel today? Mind and Body:

DAY THIRTY:

Always show more kindness than seems necessary, because the person receiving it needs it more than you will ever know ~ Unknown

Daily Meditation and Gratitude List:

Daily Fitness:

Nutritious Snacks:

Breakfast:

Lunch:

Dinner:

How do you feel today? Mind and Body:

DAY THIRTY-ONE:

If beauty comes from within, laughter is the expression of the magnificence within you. ~ Wendy Clawsey

Daily Meditation and Gratitude List:

Daily Fitness:

Nutritious Snacks:

Breakfast:

Lunch:

Dinner:

How do you feel today? Mind and Body:

RECIPES

I find the biggest challenge to eating healthy, is finding healthy food choices when I'm away from home. When I'm in Toronto, one of the only restaurants I will dine at is Fresh Restaurants. Although Fresh serves modern vegetarian food and I am not vegetarian, I don't feel like I'm missing out on anything. In fact, I feel like I hit the jackpot finding the Fresh Restaurant franchise. The food tastes amazing, it's affordable and a great alternative to traditional take-out when time is limited.

That's why I was more than thrilled when Fresh Restaurants chef Jennifer Houston and founder/owner Ruth Tal agreed to allow me to use some of her recipes to help you start eating healthy at home.

If you like her recipes and are looking for more, she has several cookbooks out. *Fresh, Refresh* and *Fresh at Home* (www.freshrestaurants.ca/cookbooks).

If you are in the Toronto area you can stop in at one of the Fresh restaurants located at 326 Bloor Street West, 894 Queen Street West, 147 Spadina Avenue or 90 Eglinton Avenue East.

As for myself I often joke that when it comes to the kitchen, I am more of a trophy wife than anything else. However, one must learn to break bread when needed. I have added a few of my own recipes that I find to be a great substitute for some of my favourite snacks and dishes.

**All ingredients should be organic and chemical free. All meat should be grass feed, antibiotic and growth hormone free. Making wise choices when you buy will insure success at home.*

Soups ... From the Kitchen of Fresh Restaurants

Vegetable Stock

(pg 20 *Refresh*)
Makes 10 cups

A good vegetable stock can make all the difference between a decent soup and an amazing soup. This vegetable stock is easy to prepare. If you can spare the time, first roast the vegetables together in the oven before you simmer them on the stove. Store-bought vegetable stock in cubes or powder is a quick and easy option. These products can be found at most natural food stores.

Ingredients

1 onion, peeled and chopped
1 carrot, peeled and chopped
1 tomato, chopped
1 cup mushrooms
1 cup parsley stems
5 garlic cloves, crushed
2 inches ginger root
6 black peppercorns
1 bay leaf
10 cups cold filtered water
sea salt, to taste

Method

1. Put all the ingredients, except salt, in a large pot and cover with cold water. Simmer for 1 hour.
2. Strain stock through a fine-mesh sieve and discard the vegetables Add sea salt to taste.
3. Store in refrigerator or in the freezer.

Butternut Squash and Pear Soup

(pg 22 *Refresh*)
Serves 6

To enhance the wonderful pear flavour in the soup, leave the pear peel on. Yellow Bosc or green Anjou pears suit this soup well. Do not use overly ripe pears.

Ingredients

1 inch ginger root, peeled and minced
1 cinnamon stick
1 butternut squash, peeled, seeded and diced
1 sweet potato, peeled and diced
6 cups Vegetable Stock (see p. 165)
1 tbsp. olive oil
1 onion, peeled and chopped
1/3 cups white wine
2 pears, cored and sliced
1/2 cup coconut milk
1 tsp. sea salt
1 tsp. white pepper
1/2 red pepper, diced

Method

1. Put the ginger, cinnamon stick, squash and sweet potato in a soup pot. Cover with vegetable stock. Bring to a boil; then reduce to a simmer.
2. While the vegetables are simmering in the soup pot, heat olive oil in frying pan. Add onion and cook until caramelized, about 5 minutes.
3. Add white wine and chopped pears to the pan. Cook for 5 minutes until wine is reduced; then add to the soup pot.

4. When the squash and sweet potatoes are cooked, about 30 minutes, add the coconut milk, salt and pepper. Remove from heat. Take out the cinnamon stick.
5. Puree in a food processor or with a hand blender. To puree in a blender, first let the soup cool; then reheat to serve. With a hand blender, you can puree while the soup is still hot.
6. Garnish with finely diced red pepper and serve.

Florentine Bean Soup

(pg 26 *Refresh*)

Serves 6

This soup is a big favourite of the Fresh Restaurants staff and customers. It is rich, flavourful and very filling, perfect for those cold winter nights served with multigrain pita. The white kidney beans should be soaked overnight in could water to cut down on their cooking time. If you haven't had the time to soak them, you may need to add more stock. Or, to make it even easier, just use canned beans; add them with the spinach at the end of cooking. If you want to substitute a different kind of cooked greens, like kale or bok choy, add them a few minutes before the soup is ready to give them time to soften.

Ingredients

2 tbsp. olive oil
1 onion peeled and chopped
3 cloves garlic, chopped
1 stalk celery, chopped
1 carrot, peeled and chopped
1/2 tsp. dried thyme
1/2 tsp. dried sage
1 pinch dried rosemary

1 pinch cayenne pepper
1 tsp. garlic powder
1/2 tsp. ground white pepper
1/3 cup dry red lentils
1/3 cup dry green lentils
1//3 cup pearl barley
1 cup dry white kidney beans (soaked overnight)
1/4 cup chopped fresh curly parsley
12 cups Vegetable Stock (see p. 165)
8 cups Spinach, chopped and loosely packed
sea salt to taste

Method

1. Heat olive oil over medium heat in a soup pot. Add the onion, garlic, celery and carrots. Sauté until soft.
2. Add the thyme, sage, rosemary, cayenne, garlic powder and white pepper, and stir.
3. Add the lentils, split peas, barley, beans, parsley and stock.

Marrakesh Curried Stew

(pg 29 *Refresh*)
Serves 6

Ruth's father was born in Marrakesh and her mother was born in Casablanca, Morocco. This is one of her original recipes, borrowed from her mother. Ruth first prepared it at her little counter at the Queen Street Market. This stew is delicious on its own, on a plate of couscous or over a bowl of brown rice.

Ingredients

2 onions, peeled and cut in chunks
2 carrots, peeled and cut in chunks

2 cups Vegetable Stock (see p. 165)
2 cups coconut milk
1 tsp. cinnamon
1/2 tsp. cayenne pepper
2 tbsp. curry powder
4 tbsp. cumin, ground
1/2 tsp. turmeric
2 white potatoes, cut in chunks
1 sweet potato, cut in chunks
1 small eggplant, cut in chunks
6 cloves garlic, minced
2 green peppers, cut in chunks
1 red pepper, cut in chunks
1 zucchini, cut in chunks
2 cups cooked or canned chick peas
3 tbsp. raisins
2 tbsp. grated coconut
sea salt to taste

Method

1. Put the onions and carrots in a large pot with 1/2 cup of vegetable stock and cook over medium heat until onion softens a bit, about 3 minutes.
2. Add the coconut mil and the spices. Cook for 1 minute, while stirring.
3. Add the white and sweet potatoes and the rest of the stock. Cover and let cook for 5 minutes.
4. Add the remaining ingredients. Stir, cover and cook until vegetables are just soft, about 20 minutes.
5. To bring out all the flavours, season to taste with a pinch or two of sea salt.

Wraps ... From the Kitchen of Fresh Restaurants

Nori Roll

(pg 48 *Refresh*)

This roll-up is great to take to work for lunch or to eat later since it keeps well unrefrigerated and won't get too soggy.

Ingredients

4 sheets toasted nori
4 cups sweet brown rice, cooked
2 cups grated carrot
2 avocados, sliced
1 pack alfalfa sprouts
1 red pepper, sliced
tamari or soy sauce for dipping
sweet brown rice, cooked (see recipe on page 181)

Method

1. Fill a small bowl with warm water. Use this water for wetting your fingers in the following steps. You can also use this water to moisten the ends of the nori so they stick together when you roll it up in step 4.
2. Lay a sheet of nori on a flat surface. Wet your fingers and spread a quarter of the rice onto the nori, leaving about an inch uncovered at the top of the sheet.
3. Place a portion of the grated carrot, avocado slices, alfalfa and red pepper horizontally about halfway down the rice.
4. Wet your fingers again and roll the nori into a thick cigar shape. Use a sharp, wet knife to cut the Nori Roll diagonally in half. Serve with tamari or soy sauce for dipping. Repeat for each serving.

Sweet Brown Rice

(pg 4 *Refresh*)
Makes 2 cups

Ingredients

1 cup sweet brown rice
1 1/2 cups filtered water
1 tsp. rice vinegar (optional)
1 tsp. maple syrup (optional)

Method

1. Rinse the rice in a saucepan and drain. A
2. dd the water and bring to a boil, then reduce to a simmer and cook, covered, for 30 minutes or until all the water has evaporated.
3. Combine the rice vinegar and maple syrup together in a small bowl and toss with the cooked rice.

Black Bean Burrito

(pg 50 *Refresh*)
Serves 4

Ingredients

4 12-inch whole wheat tortillas
2 tomatoes, diced
1 bunch cilantro, chopped
1/2 cucumber, chopped
1/2 red onion, peeled and chopped
2 cups shredded lettuce
1 batch Black Bean Filling heated
2 avocados, sliced

Method

1. Heat tortillas on a grill or in the oven.
2. Toss the diced tomato, cilantro, cucumber, red onion and lettuce together in a small mixing bowl.
3. Spread a thick layer of warm Black Bean Filling (see below) across the centre of one tortilla. Spoon on a portion of the tomato mixture. Top with avocado slices.
4. Roll the tortilla, tucking in the two ends as you go. Repeat for each serving.

Black Bean Filling

(pg 100 *Refresh*)

Makes 6 servings

Increase the amount of cayenne pepper for added spiciness. It also doubles as a filling for quesadillas or as a warm dip for corn chips.

Ingredients

6 tbsp. olive oil
2 onions, peeled and diced
4 cloves garlic, minced
2 tsp. cumin seeds, toasted and ground
1 tsp. cayenne pepper
2 tsp. apple cider vinegar
1 tsp. sea salt
4 cups canned or cooked black beans

Method

1. Heat the oil over medium heat in a saucepan. Add onions and cook for 5 minutes until soft.
2. Add the remaining ingredients except the black beans. Simmer for 5 minutes.
3. While that is cooking, puree the black beans in a food processor or mash as smoothly as possible by hand.
4. Add black beans to mixture. Stir until heated through.

Brunch ... From the Kitchen of Fresh Restaurants

Fresh Granola

(pg 114 *Refresh*)

This hearty high-protein granola is served during the Fresh Restaurants busy weekend brunches. This granola tastes delicious with all types of mild such as almond, rice, oat or soy. "Original" Flavour is best, as it is the least sweetened of the non-dairy milks. Top with a non-dairy soy yogurt and fresh berries. This granola will keep for months in an airtight container.

Ingredients

1 tbsp. sunflower oil
2 tsp. maple syrup
1/4 cup apple juice
1/4 tsp. pure vanilla extract
2 1/2 cup rolled oats
1/4 cup raw pecans, chopped
1/4 raw sunflower seeds, hulled
1/4 cup raw almonds, chopped or sliced
1 tbsp. hemp seeds, hulled
1/4 cup raw cashews, chopped
1/4 cup raw walnuts, chopped
1/8 cup shredded coconut
1/4 cup raw pumpkin seeds, hulled
1/8 cup raisins
1/8 cup currants
1/8 cup dried apricots, chopped

Method

1. Preheat oven to 350 degrees F.
2. In small bowl mix maple syrup, apple juice, vanilla and oil.
3. In large bowl mix oats, nuts, seeds and coconut. Add maple syrup mixture and toss to coat.
4. Spread mixture on a baking tray and cook until crispy, stirring often.
5. Let cool.
6. Add raisins, currants and apricots, stir and serve.

Date Purée

(pg 6 *Refresh*)
Makes 2 cups

When baking, dates are a wonderful natural sweetener to replace sugar, honey or maple syrup. They build strength and are warming to the body. See Chocolate Chip Spelt Muffins and Banana Muffins below.

Ingredients

2 1/2 cups cooking dates
2 1/2 cups filtered water
1 tbsp. vanilla extract
1/2 tsp. cinnamon
1 pinch nutmeg

Method

1. Wash and rinse the dates. Put them in a saucepan with the water, vanilla extract, cinnamon and nutmeg.
2. Cook on low heat for 25 minutes until half the water has evaporated.
3. Remove from heat and let cool.

4. When cool, place the date mixture in a good processor or blend and purée. Store in the fridge.

Chocolate Chip Spelt Muffins

(pg 119 *Refresh*)
Makes 16 muffins

These admittedly dense muffins make a delicious mid-morning or mid-afternoon snack for the active youngster or adult.

Ingredients

2 cups soymilk, plain
1 1/3 cups canola oil
2 cups Date Puree (above)
1 cup Organic dark chocolate chips
6 cups light spelt flour
4 tbsp. baking powder
1 1/2 tsp. sea salt

Method

1. Preheat oven to 325 degrees F. Lightly spray or oil two regular-sized muffin trays.
2. In a large mixing bowl, combine all the ingredients to form a batter.
3. Scoop 1/2 cup of batter per muffin onto the tray.
4. Bake for 20 to 25 minutes. Let the muffins cool for 10 minutes before removing from trays. Store at room temperature or freeze in an air-tight container.

Banana Muffins

(pg 120 *Refresh*)

Makes 16 muffins

You can substitute two cups blueberries for the bananas in this recipe. Just add four more cups of water. Ripe bananas will give you a sweeter, moister muffin.

Ingredients

2 cups rolled oats
4 cups durum flour
1 cup Date Purée (see above)
3 1/4 tbsp. baking powder
1 tsp. baking soda
1 1/2 tsp. sea salt
1 tsp. cinnamon
1/2 tsp. nutmeg
1 tsp. vanilla extract
1 cup canola oil
6 ripe bananas, mashed
2 cups water

Method

1. Preheat oven to 325 degrees F. Lightly spray or oil two regular-sized muffin trays.
2. In a large mixing bowl, combine all the ingredients to form a batter.
3. Scoop 1/2 cup of batter per muffin onto the tray.
4. Bake for 40 to 45 minutes. Let the muffins cool for 10 minutes before removing from the trays. Store at room temperature or freeze in an air-tight container.

Maple Peacan Cookies

(pg 121 *Refresh*)

Makes 32 wheat-free cookies

You can substitute walnuts or almonds for the pecans in this recipe.

Ingredients

2 1/2 cups maple syrup
1 cup canola oil
1 1/2 pecan halves
5 cups barley flour
2 tsp. cinnamon
1/2 tsp. sea salt
1/2 cup apple butter

Method

1. Combine all ingredients except the apple butter, stirring well. Add the flour gradually to avoid clumping
2. Using a teaspoon, scoop the batter in portions (a rounded teaspoon) onto a waxed cookie sheet.
3. Press your thumb into the centre of each cookie. Fill the resulting dent with a dollop of apple butter.
4. Bake for 15 to 20 minutes at 325 degree F until the cookies begin to brown. Remove from heat even if the cookies are still a bit soft; they will harden as they cool.

Fresh Fruit Smoothies ...
From the Kitchen of Fresh Restaurants

Antioxidant Smoothie
(pg 172 *Refresh*)

This slightly tart smoothie is a nice change from the mostly sweet-tasting smoothies. You can always add soymilk if you would like to sweeten it up a wee bit.

Ingredients
8 oz. bottled of organic pomegranate juice
1 banana, peeled
2 tbsp. blueberries (fresh or frozen)

Method
Place the pomegranate juice and banana in the blender. Start on a low setting while you add the blueberries. Switch to a higher setting for about a minute. Pour into a tall glass.

Susur Smoothie
(pg 174 *Refresh*)

The entire staff at Fresh Restaurants is addicted to this dazzling smoothie that is named after internationally acclaimed chef Susur Lee. Susur created this lovely combination and always requests it when he goes into Fresh Restaurant for a juice.

Ingredients
1 small beet, scrubbed
3 red apples
2 tbsp. raspberries (fresh or frozen)
6 ice cubes

Method

Juice the beet first. Follow with the apple. Place in a blender with the raspberries and ice. Start on a low setting and switch to a higher setting for about a minute. Pour into a tall glass.

Elvis Smoothie

(pg 176 *Refresh*)

This smoothie tastes just like a fabulous peanut butter, banana and jelly sandwich. This led Fresh Restaurants to Elvis Presley, who was famous for eating them all day long.

Ingredients

4 red apples
1 natural peanut butter
1 banana, peeled

Method

Juice the apples first. Place in the blender with the peanut butter and banana. Start on a low setting and switch to a higher setting for about a minute. Pour into a tall glass.

First Kiss Smoothie

(pg 177 *Refresh*)

I love that exhilarating first kiss that is so full of discovery and promise. Close your eyes when you have this smoothie and you might get something close to that sensation.

Ingredients
6 slices pineapple
3 oz. filtered water
1 banana, peeled
6 strawberries (fresh or frozen)

Method
Juice the pineapple. Add filtered water to flush the juice through. Put the pineapple juice and banana in the blender. Start on a low setting while you add the strawberries. Switch to a higher setting for about a minute. Pour into a tall glass.

All Star Salad ...
From the Kitchen of Fresh Restaurants

This is the best-selling salad on our menu, every season of the year. The combination of kale and quinoa, with the warm sweet potato and tofu steaks, is simply delicious.

You can customize the flavour with the dressing you choose. Our best selling combination is the All Star with our House Dressing (see recipe below), but this works with any dressing you can dream up.

Serves 4

4 cups	shredded kale
1 recipe	Quinoa Tabouleh (see below)
½ cup	parsley, chopped
½ cup	cilantro, chopped
3 cups	sunflower sprouts
4 tsp	goji berries
1	sweet potato cut into 8 slices (approx. 1 cm thick)
¼ cup	canola oil (for brushing on sweet potato
1 recipe	Tofu Steaks (see below)
1 recipe	Toasted Nuts & Seeds (see below)

Quinoa Tabouleh:

2 ½ cups	cooked quinoa
1/2 can	adzuki beans, drained and rinsed
1/2 cup	tomato, diced
1/4 cup	cucumber, diced
1/4 cup	parsley, chopped
2 tbsp	shelled edamame

1 tbsp	red onion, diced
3 tbsp	olive oil
4 ½ tsp	tamari

1. Mix everything together.

Grilled Sweet Potato:

Coat both sides of each slice of sweet potato with canola oil and cook in panini grill until tender. If you don't have a panini grill, cook in 350 degree oven on a cookie sheet, turning once, until tender.

Tofu Steaks:

1 250 g block firm tofu
1/2 cup tamari
2 cups water
2 tbsp ground coriander
4 tsp garlic powder

1. Cut the tofu into four slices, and then cut those slices on the diagonal to form 8 triangular steaks.
2. Mix remaining ingredients in a bowl and pour over tofu.
3. Let marinate at least an hour, or up to overnight.
4. To cook, either grill or pan fry with a little bit of canola oil over medium high heat until browned on both sides.

Toasted Nuts & Seeds:

1 tbsp each: cashews, sunflower seeds, walnuts & pumpkin seeds

Place in 350 degree oven for a few minutes until toasted. Toss once or twice. Be careful not to burn.

To assemble All Star:

1. Put 1 cup shredded kale into each of 4 large bowls.
2. Top with a quarter of the quinoa tabouleh, 2 tbsp each of the cilantro and parsley, 2 tofu steaks, 2 grilled sweet potato, ¾ cup sunflower sprouts, 1 tsp goji berries, and 1 tbsp toasted nuts & seeds.
3. Serve with dressing of your choice.

Fresh House Dressing:

1/4 cup	water
1/4 cup	apple cider vinegar
1/4 tsp	organic sugar
1 tsp	lemon juice
2 tsp	sea salt
3/4 tsp	freshly ground black pepper
3/4 tsp	tamari
1/4 tsp	mustard powder
1 clove	garlic
1/4 cup	flax oil
3/4 cup	sunflower oil

1. Put all ingredients except oil in blender and puree.
2. With blender running, add oil in a thin stream until dressing is emulsified.

From One Trophy Wife's Kitchen to Yours ... Smoothies and Juices

The Teen Approved Smoothie

Serves 2

We have no control over what our teens eat when they are out of the house; however, we can ease our minds by sending them out with a nutrient full smoothie. The taste is teen approved; in fact, my teen requests it every morning.

Ingredients

2 large kale leaves
1/2 cup baby spinach leaves
1/2 tsp. freshly ground flax seed
pinch seaweed nibs (If you have hyperthyroidism omit this step)
1 frozen organic banana (I peel and freeze ahead of time)
1/2 cup frozen blueberries (you can add any berry of your choice)
1/2 cup organic strawberries
1 tsp. raw honey
1 cup coconut milk or almond milk

Method

1. Combine all ingredients in a high power blender and blend until everything is mixed well together.
2. My teen likes to eat this smoothie thicker and with a spoon. To do this just add more frozen berries or, to sweeten it for the more fussy child, add another 1/2 a frozen banana.
3. For a smoother more liquified version add more coconut or almond milk.
4. To add extra hidden nutrients you can sneak in half a carrot and a couple broccoli florets.
5. Pour into a large glass and serve.

Ikkuma Smoothie
(www.ikkuma.com)
Serves 2

One word: AMAZING!! This has incredible body repairing, immune system boosting, gut populating, cancer fighting, age reversing, and antioxidant flooding goodness! Thanks to our friends at Ikkuma for this power house recipe. This recipe may seem daunting, but it really isn`t that hard if you stage all the ingredients.

To be staged (prepared):
"Fruit & Vegetable" Staging: Clean and chop, beets, apples, purple cabbage, broccoli, celery, ginger, kale and garlic (one clove). You can effectively use whatever vegetables you want but I stress a good variety. Chop enough for about one weeks worth of smoothies (use trial and error for this one). My experience is that chopped vegetables, placed in a sealed container with one or two paper towel sheets at the bottom, can effectively keep relatively fresh for about one week. This will save a ton of time when making your smoothies.
"Seeds of Life" Mixture: Using a coffee grinder, grind sesame, chia, and flax seeds. Place them in a small Ziploc bag and store in your freezer. Try to keep it relatively fresh by only staging two weeks worth of the mixture, though the seeds should stay fresh in the freezer for longer than that.

Ingredients
1/4 cup organic almond or coconut milk
2 cups fruit & vegetables (already prepared)
1 tbsp seeds of life mixture (already prepared)
30 grams high quality natural whey protein (or vegan protein

powder, such as sprouted brown rice, pea or hemp)
1/2 cup organic frozen berries
1 tbsp shredded coconut
2 tbsp organic yogurt (coconut yogurt can be used if you have dairy intolerance)
1/4 tsp. cinnamon to stabilize blood sugar
1/4 tsp. turmeric powder to load it with cancer fighting compounds
1 tsp. maca root powder for an energy kick (find this at any health food store)
1 tsp. glutamine for muscle repair (if desired)
fish oil (if desired)

Method
Add the following ingredients to your high powered blender and blend until desired consistency. One small caveat: if you don't have a VERY powerful blender, vegetables from the brassica (cabbage, broccoli and kale) family may promote gas. Try to introduce them slowly and if it doesn't work simply substitute with other fruits or vegetables such as spinach and avocado.

Summer Splash
Serves 1

This juice is surprisingly refreshing with a slight tang that leaves your taste buds thinking of a fresh summer's day.

Ingredients
3 carrots
1/2 stalk celery (or 1/4 cucumber)
3 fresh parsley leaves
1 apple

Method

This recipe requires a juicer. Combine all ingredients into a juicer. Pour into a large glass. I use the access pulp in sauces or as compost.

Snacks

Sweet Potato Chips

Serves 1

This is my chip substitute recipe. This tasty recipe will have your taste buds well satisfied and curve your salty cravings.

Ingredients

1 medium sweet potato; sliced, diced or cut into french-fry shape
1 tsp. fresh organic herbs & vegetable aromatic sea salt or sea salt
2 tbsp coconut oil

Method

Melt coconut oil in a large frying pan. Add sweet potato to heated coconut oil and coat. Sprinkle with seasoning. Cover with lid for approximately 10 minutes to soften the inside. (Remove lid after 10 minutes or they will be too soft.) Cook until outside is crisp and inside is soft.

A Sweet Treat; Fruit Parfait

When I'm craving something sweet, instead of reaching for the ice cream, I make a fruit parfait. Its a healthy sweet alternative that you can feel good about.

Ingredients
1 cup organic vanilla yogurt (or your favourite flavor)
2 cups your favourite fruit (banana, pineapple, berries, peaches, kiwi etc)
1 1/2 cups organic granola (I use hemp granola)
1 tsp. freshly ground flaxseed

Method
Wash and cut your fruit and place in a bowl. Pour yogurt over fruit. Add granola and flaxseed. Enjoy.

Fast Grabs

I find purchasing an assortment of fresh organic vegetables every week, washing, cutting and place them in snack size containers ahead of time gives you a healthy snack to grab on the go, instead of grabbing a bag of chips or cookies. Also keep one portion servings of hummus and other healthy dips handy.

Breakfast

Make sure when you purchase your antibiotic free, free range eggs (or chicken) that the chickens are allowed out of the chicken coop to roam. Some farmer will market their cage free chickens as free range when in fact they are jammed packed into a production house and they are simply cage free.

Veggie Eggs

This is a great way to get your veggies and your protein in.

Ingredients
2-3 organic free range, antibiotic free eggs
1 serving vegetables of your choice (asparagus, peppers etc)

Method

Heat oil or butter. Place vegetables on heated pan. Crack eggs over vegetables and place a tight fitting lid over pan. The vegetables cook in the egg and the steam will cook tops of eggs without having to flip them. Keeping your yokes intact. Add breakfast salad on the side.

Breakfast Pear Salad

This is a light and refreshing salad to start the day right.

Ingredients

10 cups baby spinach
3 ripe pears, diced into large cubes (can substitute strawberries or clementines for variety)
1/2 cup thinly sliced green onions
1/4 cup feta cheese
1/4 cup slivered almonds, toasted

Mustard Viniagrette

1/3 cup pure olive oil
3 tbsp. apple cider vinegar
1 1/2 tsp. organic sugar
1 1/2 tsp dijion mustard
1 garlic clove, mined
1/2 tsp. teaspoon sea salt

Method

In a large bowl, combine the spinach, pears, onion, cheese and almonds. In a jar with a tight-fitting lid, combine the vinaigrette ingredients; shake well. Pour over salad; toss to coat. Enjoy.

Black Beans and Eggs

This is one of my favourite breakfasts to eat when I'm visiting my family in Costa Rica, and one that I love just as equally here.

Ingredients

2-3 eggs organic free range, antibiotic free eggs
1 cup organic canned black beans
1 cup cooked brown rice (optional)
1/2 cup organic sour cream

Method

Cook your eggs as you desire. For this dish I prefer scrambled. Mix black beens and rice together. Scoop sour cream on the side.

Entrées

Bean Soup
Serves 10

This is fantastic on a cold day. I eat this soup whenever I can. The seaweed makes this soup great for anyone with hypothyroidism. (The taste of the seaweed is masked.) This recipe also freezes great. I freeze in individual servings for days when I don't have time to cook, but want something filling and hot.
**This recipe can be made with organic beans for convenience, or with dried beans soaked overnight.*

Ingredients

2 cans organic kidney beans
2 cans organic black beans
1 can organic pinto beans

1 can organic garbanzo beans
1 can organic diced tomatoes
1 stalk celery diced
1/2 onion diced
1 cup broccoli diced
1/4 cup sea weed krinkles or ground seaweed
1/2 tsp. crushed red pepper
3 fresh basil leaves
1/2 bell pepper diced

Method
Combine all ingredients into a large pot or crock pot. Cook at medium temperature for twenty minutes and then simmer for a couple hours. If you don't have the time to let it simmer cook on medium for an additional 20 minutes instead.

Tomato, Veggie and Rice Dish

This recipe tastes great and is a good way to use up vegetables that are not as fresh.

Ingredients
2 cups of diced vegetables (carrots, broccoli, collie flower, bell peppers etc)
1/2 onion chopped
2 garlic cloves minced or finally diced
2 jars of your favourite organic pasta sauce or canned tomatoes
1/2 tsp. crushed red pepper
1/2 tsp. organic oregano
1/2 tsp. organic parsley
3 fresh basil leaves (or dried organic basil)

Method

Fill a conringware dish with vegetables, onion and garlic. Pour pasta sauce or canned tomatoes over top. Add spices and stir. Cook at 350 degrees for 45 minutes. Serve over brown rice or substitute rice with ancient grain pasta.

Fajitas

This timely classic is always a favourite at my house and makes great leftovers.

Ingredients

2 tbsp canola oil
2 chicken breasts or steak cut in strips (grass fed, antibiotic-growth hormone free)
1 bell pepper chopped
1 medium onion chopped
2 garlic cloves finally diced
1/2 tsp. crushed red pepper
1/2 cup sour cream
1/2 cup salsa
1/2 cup diced tomatoes
1 cup baby spinach leaves
1/2 cup grated organic cheese
8 flaxseed, spinach or rice wraps

Method

Heat canola oil in a deep pan. Add meat to heated pan. Add crushed red pepper. Once meat is browned, add vegetables. Once fully cooked serve on wrap and top with organic sour cream, salsa, chopped tomatoes, grated cheese and spinach.

Spaghetti and Meatballs

This recipe will halt conversation, as everyone will be engrossed in eating the incredible dish you created.

Meatballs:
1 1/4 pound ground sirloin
2 tsp. worcestershire sauce
1/4 cup grated parmesan or romano cheese
2 cloves garlic chopped
1 tbsp. cumin

Method
Mix ingredients and form into large or small meatballs. Place on a nonstick cookie sheet or a cookie sheet greased with canola oil. Bake meatballs 10-12 minutes, until no longer pink (longer for larger meatballs).

Sauce:
2 tbsp. canola oil
1/2 tsp. crushed red pepper flakes
4 cloves garlic, crushed or chopped
1 small onion, finely chopped
1 can crushed tomatoes
6 chopped flat-leaf parsley
10 leaves fresh basil leaves, torn or thinly sliced

Method
Add oil, crushed pepper, garlic and finely chopped onion. Sauté 5 to 7 minutes, until onion bits are soft. Add crushed tomatoes, and herbs. Bring to a simmer and cook for about 10 minutes. Place meatballs over organic ancient grain pasta, pour sauce over and enjoy.

Fried Steak and Egg Pasta

All I can say is yummy. This new family favorite came into existence when I hadn't had a chance to grocery shopping and my ingredients were limited. But what a fantastic and tasty concoction.

Ingredients

1 steak cut in strips
1/2 onion chopped
2 cloves garlic finally diced
6 asparagus chopped
6 tbsp. canola oil
1 egg
1 tsp. crushed red pepper
1/2 tsp. parsley
1/2 tsp. oregano
1 pkg. organic ancient grain pasta
1/2 cup spinach

Method

1. On medium heat, warm half of the canola oil in deep pan or enough to line the bottom of the pan.
2. Place steak in heated oil. When meat is browned add onion, garlic, spices and mix ingredients. Add asparagus and toss.
3. Add egg and fry along with other ingredients.
4. Once all ingredients are cooked add spinach. When spinach is soften add cooked ancient grain pasta (see package for directions).
5. Pour the rest of the canola oil over pasta or enough to cover the noodles.
6. Toss all ingredients together until pasta is well mixed in and rewarmed. Serve and enjoy.

Sides

Sweet Potato and Asparagus

Serves 4

This sweet potato recipe can be converted into a side dish or a main course. By taking the sweet potato chip recipe (see p????) adding vegetables makes it a great side dish. Adding left over chicken makes it a fantastic main course and a great way to use up any leftovers.

Ingredients

3 large sweet potatoes, diced
1 tsp. fresh organic herbs & vegetable aromatic sea salt or sea salt
2 tbsp coconut oil
5 asparagus chopped (you can substitute bell peppers, broccoli or other vegetables of your choice)

Method

1. Melt coconut oil in a large frying pan.
2. Add sweet potato to heated coconut oil and coat. Sprinkle with seasoning.
3. Add chopped asparagus or other dense vegetables (if using bell peppers wait until lid is removed to add).
4. Cover with lid for approximately 10 minutes to soften the inside. Remove lid after ten minutes or they will be too soft.
5. *If you would like to make this into a meal, add leftover chicken shortly after removing lid.*
6. Cook until sweet potatoes are crisp on the outside and soft on

TIP: For those of you on the road. A lunch bag with snack sized fruit and vegetables, plus a bottle of water, will help avoid having to stop for fast food or unhealthy snacks throughout the day.

TIP: I also keep an organic chocolate bar in my purse at all times. Whenever you have a craving, take a piece of chocolate and let it melt in your mouth, savouring every second of that little piece of chocolate delight, to nip the craving at your taste buds.

IN CONCLUSION

The Dalai Lama, when asked what surprised him most about humanity, answered "Man. Because he sacrifices his health in order to make money. Then he sacrifices money to recuperate his health. And then he is so anxious about the future that he does not enjoy the present; the result being that he does not live in the present or the future; he lives as if he is never going to die, and then dies having never really lived."

Rest, play and work equally. Remembering to live for the day, while enjoying each moment.

RECOMMENDED READING

Ikkuma: Evolution Of Vitality by Gary LeBlanc

Maximized Living Nutrition Plans, The Solution To Dangers Of Modern Nutrition by B.J. Hrdick, Kimberly Roberto, Ben Lerner

Transdermal Magnesium Therapy by Dr. Mark Sircus

The Magnesium Miracle by Carolyn Dean, M.D., N.D.